A GUIDE TO THE MUSIC
OF THE EASTERN ORTHODOX CHURCH

A GUIDE TO THE MUSIC OF THE EASTERN ORTHODOX CHURCH

by

N. Lungu, G. Costea, and I. Croitoru

Translated and edited by

Nicholas K. Apostola

Holy Cross Orthodox Press
Brookline, Massachusetts
1984

Funds toward the publication of this book were provided
by the **ARCHBISHOP IAKOVOS EDUCATION FUND**.

Published by Holy Cross Orthodox Press
50 Goddard Avenue
Brookline, Massachusetts 02146

Cover design by **Mary C. Vaporis**

Library of Congress Cataloging in Publication Data

Lungu, N.
    A guide to the music of the Eastern Orthodox Church.

    English version of: Gramatica muzicii psaltice.
    1. Church music—Orthodox Eastern Church.
I. Costea, G. II. Croitoru, I. III. Title.
ML3060.L8613 1984   7838.02'619   84-10847
ISBN 0-917651-00-6 (pbk.)

Profesor N. LUNGU
Preot Prof. GR. COSTEA   Profesor I. CROITORU

GRAMATICA MUZICII PSALTICE

STUDIU COMPARATIV CU NOTAȚIA LINIARĂ

Tipărită cu aprobarea Sfîntului Sinod
și cu binecuvîntarea Prea Fericitului

JUSTINIAN
PATRIARHUL BISERICII ORTODOXE ROMÂNE

EDIȚIA DOUA

BUCUREȘTI
EDITURA INSTITUTULUI BIBLIC ȘI DE MISIUNE ORTODOXĂ
1 9 6 9

CONTENTS

FOREWORD TO THE ROMANIAN EDITION

The traditional music of our Church, the music to which the Romanian people were introduced along with Christianity, has its origins in the same part of the Middle East that was also the cradle of Christianity. It was originally transmitted to us through the oral tradition, and then later through the written tradition.

Psaltic musical writing or notation has its beginnings in the ekphonic semiography of the first Christian centuries, a simple notation which was used only for the singing of the Gospels and Epistles. This semiography, through its augmentation and enrichment by other signs, gave birth to two other semiographies: The Constantinopolitan, which the Russians adopted in the 10th century when they were converted to Christianity, and the Aghiopolitan, whose author is St. John of Damascus.

Because it was well organized and sufficiently complete, the notation of St. John of Damascus asserted itself, being in use for several centuries. It also passed through many modifications and reforms which both added and simplified signs. It was further modified in the 19th century when three great Orthodox teachers: Chrisanthos Metropolitan of Dyrachion, Gregorios Protopsaltis, and Hurmuzios the Chartophilax (Archivist) established a new system of musical notation, rendered into Romanian through the work of the Protopsaltis Macarie the Hieromonk, and the talented Anton Pann. They were succeeded by an entire line of other skillful Romanian protopsaltes.

Bucharest became at the beginning of the 19th century the most important center for ecclesiastical music. Peter Ephesios published the first book in all of Orthodoxy of psaltic music here. It was here that the great protopsaltes of Constantinople and Greece found unlimited support for the development of this music. And it is also here where the greatest number of books concerned with the theory and practice of psaltic music are found today.

It should be added that all the effort of the various reformers of
psaltic notation was to make this notation easily understood and therefore
accessible to the general public. They will not then have succeeded if
its use remains only with the specialists, who have studied this music
over a long period of time, either in seminaries, or different schools
of ecclesiastical music attached to Episcopates and monasteries (which
after the appropriation of the monasteries' holdings have become rare).
It naturally follows, that faced with the fear that psaltic notation
would no longer be able to be understood, we should attempt to transcribe
psaltic notation into linear notation.

To accomplish this transcription (initiated for the first time in 1882
by Bishop Melchisedek of Roman) and to accomplish the desire of His Beatitude Patriarch Justinian to uniformize the Romanian ecclesiastical melodies
through the composition of a manual of uniform ecclesiastical melodies, the
Holy Synod established a commission of renown professors of both psaltic
and liniar music to proceed first to systematize--through a grammar book
more indepth and complete than previous ones--the precise theoretical rules
which would permit the uniform execution of the melodies, and after that
to begin on uniform manuals of church hymns.

The result of the work of the commission composed of Prof. N. Lungu,
Rev. Prof. Gr. Costea and Prof. Ion Croitoru, can be seen in this work:
The Grammar of the Psaltic Music of the Church: a comparitive study with
liniar music. In addition, in the appendix, there is the Orthography of
Psaltic Music by Macarie and Anton Pann. This entire work has been published with the approval of the Holy Synod and the blessings of His Beatitude Patriarch Justinian by the Press of the Bible and Mission Institute
in the year 1951. In the preface of these editions the authors have presented in large part the principles with which they began, the difficulties
which they encountered and the methods which they used to overcome them.

FOREWORD TO THE ROMANIAN EDITION

This book is republished for a second time by the direction and guidance of His Beatitude Patriarch Justinian in order to make this, as everything, a true altar of faith, and so that these songs of praise and prayer may be raised. And, in order that we may continue to the end of the road on which we began, we present this book of Psaltic Music Theory.

The Press of the Bible and

Mission Institute

INTRODUCTION TO THE ENGLISH EDITION

The study of Psaltic, or, as it is known more commonly here in the west, Byzantine Music, has been hampered by the inavailability of texts in English. In addition, Byzantine Music itself presents difficulties because it is not simply a different set of melodies which are based on current musical theory, rather, it is itself an entire musical system based on distinct and unique premises. Therefore, the student of Byzantine Music, the music of the Holy Orthodox Church, confronts serious obstacles in his or her attempt to carry on the musical tradition of the Church. It is with regard for the need of a coherent text on Byzantine Music Theory and for the need to adapt the traditional music of the Church to the current situation that this book is presented.

In the Forward to the Romanian edition of this book, the authors wrote: "They will not then have succeeded if its [Byzantine Music's] use remains only with the specialists, who have studied this music over a long period of time." And, "It naturally follows, that faced with the fear that psaltic notation would no longer be able to be understood, we should attempt to transcribe psaltic notation into linear notation." The concern of the Romanian commission who compiled and wrote this book remains our concern. That is why I undertook to translate this book from the Romanian and edit it for its most effective use for our situation in America.

Byzantine Music will fall into disuse if serious measures are not taken. It is the opinion of some that this would be of little consequence. But before we elect to discard an important piece of our tradition, we should take a closer look at why this specific form of music was chosen, and what the result would be if, by default, we choose another form of music which may be less suitable for use by the Church. The ancients understood that music was not necessarily benign. That is evident in the way they descibe music theory. And the Fathers of the Church chose only eight modes or tones (ihoi), from the many which existed, for use in the Church. Others were rejected because they were seen to have a negative effect on the disposition of the soul for prayer and even encouraged the passions. We can see that same truth at work today. Is there any doubt that the structure, rhythm, and melodies of rock music heighten what is referred to in the spiritual realm as the fleshly passions? Music, all kinds of music, affects the soul in ways that are barely perceived by those of us whose spiritual eyes are clouded over by the cares of this world. If then, the Church is the means by which we are shaped into spiritual beings, as we Orthodox Christians believe, we must be extroadinarily careful about such an important medium as music and how it is used in the Church.

This is not to say that Byzantine Music in every detail is absolutely adaptable to the current situation of the Church especially in the diaspora. There will be some modifications necessary. For example, throughout the text in the sections on the theories of each tone, there are examples of hymns for that tone. What I did was to preserve the melody by manipulating the words to fit the music. This is not good Byzantine Music. In Byzantine Music the words are primary. If a hymn does not make sense in the language in which it is being sung, then it does not matter how beautiful the melody is. The music is there to serve the words; the words do not serve the music. This is theology, not simply 'taste.' The human person is first 'logical' or 'rational' being created in the image and likeness of God. The words of the hymn are the means by which we contemplate God, pray to God, and learn about God. The music is but a 'skin,' if you will, surrounding the words of the hymn. Unfortunately, creating both the best translations of the hymns and the most effective melody for the hymn requires generations of effort and is beyond the scope of this work. This book's first purpose is music theory, and therefore, I sacrificed absolute purity of

INTRODUCTION

translation for the sake of the music.

Now lest we think that creating beautiful and poetic translations of the magnificent hymns of our Church and remaining faithful to traditional Byzantine melodies is impossible in English, I should like to remind you that this book is translated from the Romanian. The Romanians use Byzantine Music. They have even translated the various prosomia to fit the traditional Byzantine prologues (pattern melodies). I am continually amazed at how faithful they have been to both the words of the hymns and the music. And it is a source of courage for me that it is possible to transmit through the English language both the wealth of Orthodox hymnography and the beauty of Byzantine Music. But theirs was a process that took hundreds of years with generations of translators, one improving on the other. It was a process of the Church not of individuals, because the Church as a whole was committed to the transmission of the faith in the native language. I might also observe here that this process of translation has not stopped. Each new edition of the various liturgical books is reviewed by a commission appointed by the Patriarch, ensuring that the translations remain faithful to both the original language and the current usage in the Romanian vernacular. Therefore there has been no evolution of a Liturgical Romanian as we have seen in the Greek or in the Slavonic. The language of the Church is truly the language of the people.

This book then is offered not as the last word on the subject, but as a first step in the long pilgrimage of making Orthodoxy comfortable in America, as comfortable as we can ever be in our earthly sojourn to the Kingdom of Heaven.

Rev. Fr. Nicholas K. Apostola

Epiphany, 1984

SOME GENERAL COMMENTS ABOUT MUSIC

Music is an art. It concerns itself with the study of musical sounds.

A musical sound is any sound which pleases the ear, except for noise, which is not pleasing and with which the art of music does not occupy itself.

The Properties of Musical Sound. There are four properties of musical sounds, called: pitch, duration, strength or intensity, and timbre, that is to say the specific musical quality of each voice or of each musical instrument.

The Name of the Musical Sounds. We distinguish in the psaltic music of the Church between seven different sounds called: Ni, Pa, Vou, Ga, Di, Ke, and Zo, which correspond in western liniar notation to: Do, Re, Mi, Fa, Sol, La, and Ti.

The Writing of Musical Sounds. All musical sounds can be shown in writing through specific musical signs, in the same manner that spoken words can be shown through letters.

Musical Scale. When musical sounds represented by the seven names are linked together progressively, that is in the order of the pitches--either ascending or descending--with the repetition of the sound from the beginning, it forms that which we call a musical scale.

Here is the scale, both ascending and descending:

Ascending:

Ni, Pa, Vou, Ga, Di, Ke, Zo, Ni

Do, Re, Mi, Fa, Sol, La, Ti, Do

Descending:

Ni, Zo, Ke, Di, Ga, Vou, Pa, Ni

Do, Ti, La, Sol, Fa, Mi, Re, Do

Here is the Scale graphically:

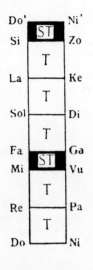

Exercise:

Do an exercise by reading and singing the sounds of the steps both up and down the scale, with the psaltic and liniar names, shown here, using the following example:

1. Ni-Pa-Ni (Do-Re-Do)

2. Ni-Pa-Vou-Pa-Ni (Do-Re-Mi-Re-Do)

3. Ni-Pa-Vou-Ga-Vu-Pa-Ni (Do-Re-Mi-Fa-Mi-Re-Do)

4. Ni-Pa-Vou-Ga-Di-Ga-Vou-Pa-Ni (Do-Re-Mi-Fa-Sol-Fa-Mi-Re-Do)

5. Ni-Pa-Vou-Ga-Di-Ke-Di-Ga-Vou-Pa-Ni- (Do-Re-Mi-Fa-Sol-La, etc.)

6. Ni-Pa-Vou-Ga-Di-Ke-Zo-Ke-Di-Ga-Vou-Pa-Ni (Do-Re-Mi, etc.)

7. Ni-Pa-Vou-Ga-Di-Ke-Zo-Ni-Zo-Ke-Di-Ga-Vou-Pa-Ni (Do-Re-Mi, etc.)

Musical Signs

In the psaltic music of the Church we distinguish between four kinds of musical signs: Vocal, Temporal, Consonant and Phthoral.

The Vocal signs are those which serve to show us in writing the different distances of ascent or descent in singing. There are a total of ten signs of which there are five of ascent, four of descent, and one which neither ascends nor descends but maintains the preceding sound.

⌣   Ison. This neither ascends nor descends, but repeats the sound

before it.

━   Oligon. Ascends one step (a second).

⌣   Petasti. Ascends one step, and is sung with an accent (a second).

ᵥᵥ   Kentima. Ascends one step, and is sung softer without an accent

(a second).

˙   Kentima. Ascends two steps transgressively (a third).

✓   Ipsili. Ascends four steps transgressively (from one step to its

fifth, i.e., a fifth).

TE 1:

The kentimata (ᵥᵥ) can be written either alone, or it can be written

ove or below an oligon. In this case it represents two ascending steps

ng in sequence (i.e., the oligon one sound, the kentimata another sound).

e sign which is below is sung first, then the other sign is sung.

NOTE 2a:

The kentimata is always sung together with the proceding vocal sign (ex. a).

NOTE 2b:

When it is accompanied by a text, it does not receive a new syllable, rather it elongates the syllable of the word written under the preceeding note (ex. b).

O - Lord

NOTE 3:

The distance between a given note on a given step of the scale, and another note is called an interval. Intervals take their name from the number of steps which they comprise, taking into account the step from which we leave to the step on which we arrive. Take, for example, the following intervals: a second 1-2 Ni-Pa (Do-Re); a third 1-3 = Ni-Vou (Do-Mi); a fourth 1-4 = Ni-Ga (Do-Fa); a fifth 1-5 = Ni-Di (Do-Sol); a sixth 1-6 = Ni-Ke (Do-La); a seventh 1-7 = Ni-Zo (Do-Ti); and an octave 1-8 = Ni-Ni (Do-Do).

NOTE 4:

In psaltic music, calculation of vocal signs, whether ascending or descending, does not take into account the step from which ones leaves. The computation begins with the step immediately above, if it is an ascending interval, or immediately below, if it is a descending interval. This will be seen more clearly in the chapter on intervals.

The Vocal Signs of Descent

⤳ Apostrophos. This descends one step (a second).

Ex.:

♪ Hyporoe. Descends two steps, one after the other.

Ex.:

⌒ Elaphron. Descends two steps transgressively, that is from one step to the third (a third).

Ex.:

Hamili. Descends four steps transgressively, that is from one step to the fifth (a fifth).

Ex.:

NOTE:

The hyporoe, like the kentimata, is sung together with the preceding note, elongating the syllable under that note, if there is a text.

EXAMPLES FOR SINGING THE SIMPLE VOCAL SIGNS

Note: Each vocal sign has
the duration of one beat.

Other Exercises without the Kentima or Ipsili

Note:

In the exercises learned up until now, we have observed that the ✎ (kentima) and 🗸 (ipsili) have not been used. This is because these two vocal signs are not written alone, but only in conjunction with either an oligon or petasti, in which case the oligon or petasti, as auxiliary signs, do not enter into the calculation of the distance between notes.

For example: a)➤➤ or ➤ , the kentima when located at or under the
right end of an oligon ascends two steps transgressively (1-3) with the
oligon simply serving as an auxiliary.

Example:

b) ⌣ or ⌣ , the ipsili located at either the right end or the
middle of the oligon or petasti ascends four steps transgressively (1-5)
with the oligon or petasti simply serving as auxiliaries.

Example:

In the same way the oligon and petasti can also serve to assist
the ison, and all the vocal signs of descent. In which case they are
sung with an accentuation.

Example: ⌣⌣; ⌣⌣; ⌣⌣; ⌣⌣; ⌣⌣.

Exercises for writing, reading and singing the above vocal signs both
simply and compound

Exercise: 1) Ni-Pa-Ni-Pa-Vu-Pa-Vu // 2) Pa-Ni-Pa-Vu-Ga-Pa-Ga.
             3) Vu-Pa-Vu-Ga-Di-Vu-Di // 4) Ga-Vu-Ga-Di-Ke-Ga-Ni.
             5) Ni-Zo-Ke-Di-Ke-Zo-Di // 6) Zo-Ke-Di-Ga-Di-Ke-Ga.
             7) Di-Ga-Vu-Pa-Vu-Ga-Pa // 8) Ga-Vu-Pa-Ni-Di-Di-Ni.

Note: In order to become fully acquainted with psaltic music, signs, especially in comparison with liniar notation, exercises such as these are invaluable. Therefore they will be employed frequently.

Recapitulative exercise of reading and singing applying all the signs
learned up until now including those assisted by the oligon and petasti

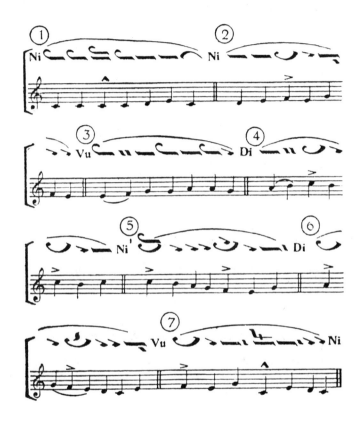

Note: One should sing the notes very carefully, executing them in a proper manner. One should avoid haste.

TEMPORAL SIGNS

In the exercises up until now, each vocal sign has had the duration
of one beat. That is to say the time it takes to drop and lift the hand.
There are hymns which require that some of the sounds be longer or
shorter than one beat. In these cases we have signs which are placed next
to the vocal signs called temporal signs. For the time being we will use
only two of these signs, namely:

1)   The clasma, ⟶ which is placed above or below a vocal sign
and which causes each sound represented by that sign to be extended
by an additional beat.

Example:

NOTE: When the clasma appears written below the petasti thusly (⌣),
the effect is not only to extend the duration of the note another beat,
but also to produce an accentuated modulation ascending to the step immediately above it in the first beat, then, in the second beat, returning
to the note from which one left.   Example:

2)   The Gorgon (⌐), which is placed above or below a given note
and which causes the note to be executed in the time it takes to lift the
hand, shortening thenote preceeding it by one-half a beat.

Example:

13

NOTE 1: When the gorgon is located on an oligon, which has a kentimata above or below it, the gorgon always refers to the kentimata, which is sung together with the preceding note in one beat.

Example:

NOTE 2: When the gorgon is placed above an hyporoe (𝄺), it causes the first descending note of the hyporoe to be sung in one beat together with the preceding note.

Example:

NOTE 3: When an apostrophos is immediately followed by an elaphron (⌐) the apostrophos is sung as though it had a gorgon above it, while the elaphron descends only one step, instead of two steps transgressively. This is called the continuous elaphron.

Example:

14

NOTE 4: When an elaphron, which follows an apostrophos, is located at a greater distance or is separated by a comma, then the apostrophos descends one step, and the elaphron descends two, each retaining one whole beat.

Example:

EXERCISES, Applying the clasma and the gorgon

A.   Clasma; the gorgon above the hyporoe and the oligon with a kentimata

B. Petasti with a clasma, and the continuous elaphron (⌣ ; ⌐)

NOTE: In executing these exercises use the psaltic as well as the
liniar names of the note, keeping in mind, as much as possible,
musical phrasiology.

C. Recapitulative exercises using the temporal signs learned up
    until now.

COMBINATIONS OF VARIOUS VOCAL SIGNS

In the hymns which we will be learning we will encounter a variety
of intervals, some greater and some smaller than those with which we
are already acquainted.

These intervals are created with the assistance of those vocal signs
already learned which can be combined in different ways in order to give
us the possibility to ascend or descend how ever much is necessary to
execute the melody formed from this kind of interval. Most of the vocal
signs we know we will also find in combination with, or as an auxiliary
to the oligon or petasti.

Here is a listing of the combinations.

Combination Signs of Ascent:

Petasti combined with an oligon ascends
two steps transgressively (a third)

An oligon or petasti combined with a
kentima ascends three steps transgressively (a fourth)

An ipsili, when located at the right
end or middle of an oligon or petasti,
ascends four steps transgressively
(a fifth)

An ipsili, when located at the left end
of an oligon or petasti, ascends five
steps transgressively (a sixth)

18

or   A kentima in combination with an ipsili when using the oligon or petasti as an auxiliary ascends six steps transgressively (a seventh)

or   An oligon or petasti, combined with a kentima and ipsili ascends seven steps transgressively (an octave)

or   Two ipsiles combined and located above a oligon or petasti ascend eight steps transgressively (a ninth)

And so forth.

Combination Signs of Descent:

An elaphron combined with an apostrophos descends three steps transgressively (a fourth)

A hamili combined with an apostrophos descends five steps transgressively (a sixth)

A hamili combined with an elaphron descends six steps transgressively (a seventh)

A hamili combined with an elaphron and an apostrophos descends seven steps transgressively (an octave)

Two hamilies combined descend eight steps transgressively (a ninth).

And so forth.

Combination and Assorted Signs of Descent

An apostrophos assisted by an oligon
or petasti descends one step accentuated
(a second)

An hyporoe assisted by an oligon or petasti
descends two steps one after the other
(seconds)

An elaphron assisted by an oligon or
petesti descends two steps transgressively
(a third)

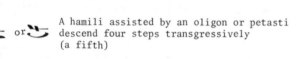

An elaphron combined with an apostrophos
and assisted by an oligon or petasti
descends three steps transgressively
(a fourth)

A hamili assisted by an oligon or petasti
descend four steps transgressively
(a fifth)

A hamili combined with an apostrophos and
assisted by an oligon or petasti descends
five steps transgressively (a sixth)

A hamili combined with an elaphron and
assisted by an oligon or petasti
descends six steps transgressively
(a seventh)

A hamili combined with an elaphron and
an apostrophos and assisted either by an
oligon or pestasti descends seven steps
transgressively (an octave)

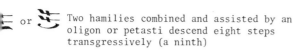 Two hamilies combined and assisted by an oligon or petasti descend eight steps transgressively (a ninth)

And so forth.

NOTE 1: ‿ The ison, in like manner, can be assisted by either the oligon or petasti.

NOTE 2: In psaltic music, the computation of the vocal signs or ascent or descent, be they simple, combined, or assisted, begins with the next step. For this reason, the step from which we leave should also be added, to the number of steps which form an interval, as in liniar notation.

Example:

Explanation: The ipsili, located on the right side of the petasti ascends four steps. In its ascent from Ni to Di (Do to Sol) it has formed an interval of a fifth resulting from those four steps: (Pa, Vou, Ga, Di (Re, Mi, Fa, Sol) to which we add Ni (Do), the step from which we left.

A General Rule: Vocal signs assisted by an oligon or petasti are sung more accentuatedly.

EXAMPLES OF ASCENDING AND DESCENDING INTERVALS

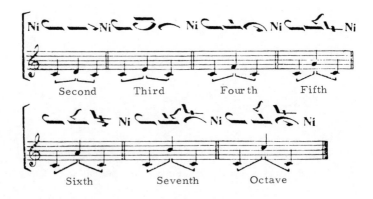

Note: Inasmuch as psaltic notation lacks the lines and spaces of a staff which show the location of the notes, the interval's intonation, and the mental calculation of the number of transgressive steps which form the interval, it requires much more attention, as compared to liniar notation, when executing intervals. For this reason it is recommended that the above section on intervals be stressed and be returned to frequently until one acquires a definite skill at intoning them.

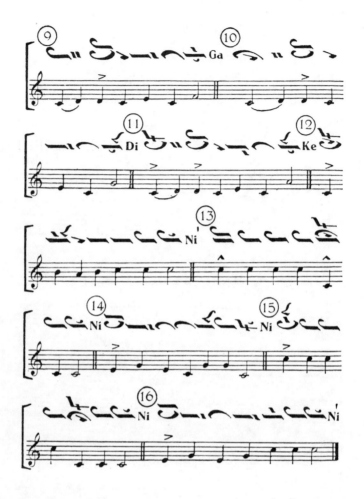

Note: These exercises should first be read and only after they have been
learned well should they be sung.

TONE, SEMI-TONE, AND TETRACORD

We have seen that the musical scale which begins with Ni (Do), is composed of eight steps. (Observe the scale below):

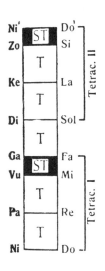

Singing anew the sounds of this scale, in ascent and descent, we notice that all the distances between the notes are not the same. For example, we can observe that between Vou-Ga (Mi-Fa) and Zo-Ni (Ti-Do) the distances heard are much smaller. Therefore, we have two kinds of distances: five larger which we call tones and two smaller which we call semi-tones.

Looking at the construction of this scale we see that it is composed of two prefectly equal parts (Ni-Ga; Do-Fa and Di-Ni; Sol-Do) divided by the distance of one tone (Ga-Di; Fa-Sol).

Both the bottom and top parts of the scale are formed by four steps. Each of these parts is called a tetracord (four-step). We have, therefore, a lower and upper tetracord, divided by the distance of one tone.

NOTE: Sing the scale many times, both ascending and descending, observing the tones, and semi-tones as well as the tetracords.

DISDIAPASONATE SCALE

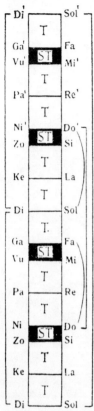

Inasmuch as we will encounter in different ecclestastical hymns sounds that will go beyond high Ni and below low Ni it is necessary that the scale with which we have been familiar until present be expanded beyond high Ni by fourstep to Di (Sol) and likewise to be expanded beyond low Ni to Di (Sol). In this way we obtain a double-scale which begins with low Di (Sol) and goes to Di (Sol) above high Ni.

This double-scale is called the Disdiapasonate Scale.

Note: Sing this disdiapasonate scale many times up and down, observing its structure and scope; you will learn the foundation of the diatonic scale from low Ni (Do) to high Ni (Do).

OTHER TEMPORAL SIGNS

Apli = •   As distinguished from the clasma, it adds one simple beat to the note under which it is written.

Dipli = ••   It is a composite of the apli which adds two beats to the note under which it is written.

Tripli = •••   It is also a composite of the apli which adds three beats to the note under which it is written. The apli and those signs composed from it have additional uses which we will see later.

Argon ⌐ . Is placed only above an oligon which has a kentimata under it. It causes the kentimata to be sung in the time it takes to lift the hand, as though it had a gorgon above it; and the oligon is lengthened by another beat as though it had a clasma above it.

Example:

Diargon has the same effect as the argon except that the oligon's duration is lengthened by two beats.

Example:

Exercise Applying the Temporal Signs: Argon and Diargon

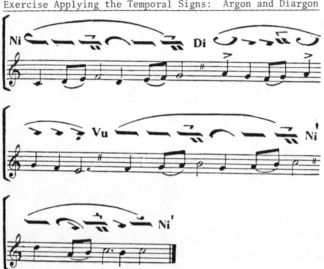

Digorgon Is a composite of the gorgon which causes three notes to be sung in one beat. It is placed on the middle of the group of the three notes. In liniar notation it corresponds to a triplet

Example:

<u>Trigorgon</u> - ⌒ It also is a composite of the gorgon which causes four notes to be sung in one beat. It is placed on the second note of the group of four notes. It corresponds to sixteenth notes in liniar notation.

Example:

<u>Exercises Applying the Temporal Signs: Digorgon and Trigorgon</u>

Stavros (cross) = ✢ It is a symbol in the form of a cross and which is written after a note which is of no longer duration than a beat. It is used to interrupt the singing for a short breath (i.e., a breath mark)

Example:

The Punctuated Gorgon

We have become familiar with the two temporal signs apli and gorgon and their composites and how each works. But here below we now see the different uses of the apli and the dipli in conjunction with the gorgon:

1. Apli before a gorgon, like this

2. Apli following a gorgon, like this

3. Dipli before a gorgon, like this

4. Dipli following a gorgon, like this

5. Apli before a digorgon, like this

6. Apli following a digorgon, like this

7. Apli in the middle of a digorgon  syncope

8. Apli in the following formula
   as it is most frequently used

RECAPITULATIVE EXERCISES

Note: The above exercises are given only to acquaint you with the technique of rythym.

Rests in Psaltic Music

In order to show the various rests that one will meet in singing psaltic music, we make use of the temporal signs: the apli and its composites, the dipli, and tripli, and the gorgon, each preceeded by a sign called the varia (⟍) which we will meet again in another chapter.

Rest Signs

A one beat rest (in liniar notation, a quarter rest) is expressed by a varia followed by an apli. Example:

A two beat rest (a half rest) is expressed by a varia followed by a dipli. Example:

A three beat rest (a half and quarter rest) is expressed by a varia followed by a tripli. Example:

A four beat rest (a whole rest) is expressed by a varia followed by a tetrapli. Example:

A half-beat rest (an eight rest) is expressed by a varia followed by an apli with a gorgon preceeded by a vocal sign. Example:

A sixteenth rest. Example:

Consonants: Signs of Expression and Ornament

The consonants are various signs, which are written next to the vocal signs, and which give them a particular expression in singing.

There are five symbols in all and called:

1. Varia = ⟍ which in addition to the use with which we are already familiar, also fulfills the function of a consonant in the following ways:

A. When it is located before a vocal sign which as the duration of one beat, it causes that note to be executed with a certain raising of the voice going up to the note immediately above and returning to the note from which you left.

Example:

B. Before a note of which has the duration of one-half beat (being effected by a gorgon), the varia simply produces an accent.

Example:

NOTE: The same effect is produced by a varia on notes of one beat, but only when they are part of a hymn which has a lively tempo (irmologica).

C. In the following melodic formula, which is encountered frequently, the varia is executed in this way:

Example:

NOTE: When the varia is followed by an ison with an apostrophos below it, like this 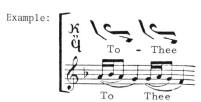 , then the ison, with the effect of the varia, is sung first, then the apostrophos elongating the syllabel of the text underneath the ison.

Example:

2. Omalon = ⟶ It is usually written under two or three notes representing the same sound, and causes the tie between the notes to be sung with a rapid undulation, crescendoing to the step immediately above and returning again lightly to the initial sound.

The omalon in this case is preceeded by a varia (∖) which replaces the accent of a clasma transformed into an ison.

Example:

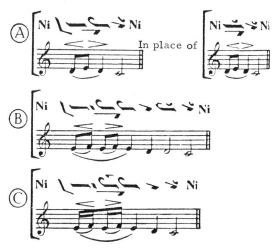

35

The omalon can also be placed under a single note, but in this case it must have either a clasma (Ex. A) or an argon (Ex. B). However, it is no longer preceeded by a varia.

Examples:

 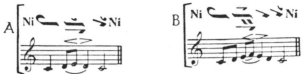

NOTE: Exceptions to this rule occur in the formula of the final cadence of the "Glory Dogmatikon" of the Tone V and of the "Glories" stihirarica o Tone V where a note with an omolon has neither a clasma nor an argon.

Example:

3.   Antikenoma = ⌐→ Cause the note under which it is placed to be sung with an ascent more lively than the tempo, in comparison with the other consonants.

We find it most frequently used in the following ways:

A.   Under a vocal sign with an apli: etc.).

Example:

B.   Under an oligon without an apli and without a gorgon:

NOTE: ♭ This symbol causes the intonation of the note to descend by a semi-tone (i.e., a flat).

C.   Under an oligon with a gorgon, in which case, on account of the gorgon, the function of the antikenoma is reduced to a small crescendo.

Example:

D.   In the melodic formula below, frequently used in the various cadences, the antikenoma in conjunction with the varia produces the following effect:

a)   Example:

NOTE: This is the correct transcription, but it can be executed only by a single chanter, and not by a group.

b)   Example:

NOTE: The effect of the antikenoma simplified and reduced to a small cresendo. This is the preferred version.

4.   Psifiston = ‿ It is usually written under either an ison or an oligon, and all of their combinations. It gives a strong accent in the form of a grace note to the note under which it is written. Two or more descending notes must follow it. The psifiston is used in the following three cases:

A.   Placed under a note which has the duration of one beat, the psifiston causes this note to be sung accentuatedly and to be preceeded by another note of short duration, located on the step immediately above. In liniar notation, this note of short duration which preceeds the real note under which the psifiston is written is called a grace note.

Example:

B.   Placed under a note which is followed by an apostrophos with a gorgon, that is, having the duration of one-half a beat, the psifiston has the same effect as in the first case.

Example:

C.   Placed under a note which as a clasma, the psifiston causes this note to be sung with energy and to be proceeded by another note, which has the duration of a half beat, located on the step immediately above. In this case, the effect of the psifiston gives much expression to the hymn.

Example:

5.   Eteron = ⌒ It is written under two or more notes on the same step or on different steps, causing these notes to be sung uninterruptedly, that is in a single breath, in the following manner:

A.   When the eteron is placed under two or more notes on different steps, it causes these notes to be sung in a single breath (a tie), having in this manner the function of a legato in liniar notation.

Example:

B.   When the eteron unites two notes on the same step, be they alone or in a group with other kinds of notes, the similar notes (those on the same step) are sung with a slight undulation upward.

Example:

C.   Placed under a single note which has a dipli or tripli and is preceeded by a varia, the eteron causes the note to be elongated without a breath, and having on the penultimate beat the effect of an antikenoma with an apli.

Example:

EXERCISES USING THE CONSONANTS (Signs of Ornamentation)

PSIFISTON

Note: a) Note well the effect of the antikenoma in conjunction with the varia.

b) Similarly, note the effect of the psifiston on notes with greater and lesser value (the kind of grace notes).

ETERON = ⌒

Note: a) Consonants in psaltic music correspond to signs of ornamentation in liniar notation and enrich and beautify the melody when they are placed along side the vocal signs.

In order to see this in action, and to verify the correct execution of the ornamentation, that is the consonants, it is recommendable to sing the melody with only the vocal signs, as though the consonants were not there, and then to sign it using the consonants.

CONCERNING TEMPO

The pace used in the execution of a song is called tempo.

In psaltic music there are four types of tempo; called:

1. Papadica (Adagio, Largo) which is represented by a "T"
with a digorgon above it ($\overset{\text{\tiny \`}}{T}$) and which indicates a very
slow tempo, and is used especially in heruvika and koinonika.

2. Stihirarica (Andante, Larghetto) which is represented by
a "T" with an argon above it ($\overset{\smile}{T}$) and indicates a tempo slightly
faster than the papadica. The stihi, the doxastika and the
Axions, are sung in this tempo.

3. Irmologica (Moderato and Allegretto), which is represented
by a "T" with a gorgon above it ($\overset{\frown}{T}$), is used in the following
ways:

    a) Moderato in which are generally sung the troparia

    (Apolotykia) of the Resurrection, of the feasts, of the

    saints, the irmoi of the canons, and other hymns of Vespers

    and Matins which are found in this tempo.

    b) Allegretto, a variant in this same irmologica tempo

    in which generally are sung the Katavasia, the troparia of

    the canons, and other hymns appropriate to this tempo.

4. Recitative which is represented by a "T" with a digorgon
above it ($\overset{\varsigma}{T}$) and indicates that it should be executed as
though singing the spoken word (recitativo).

Signs of Alteration (Accidents)

In psaltic music we use two signs of alteration called diesis (δ) which located under a note causes it to be raised by a semitone, and an hyphesis (ρ) which located above a note causes it to be lowered by a semitone. These two accidentals of ecclesiastical music correspond in liniar notiaton to a sharp and flat. The diesis (σ) and hyphesis (ρ) have influence only on the notes upon which they are located, not on other similar notes which might follow.

Example:

NOTE: We do not have in psaltic music a special sign which returns the altered note, to its natural intonation, as we have a natural sign in liniar notation. For this function we have certain signs called phthorai about which we will speak in a future chapter. Otherwise, in this musical system, the effect of the diesis and hyphesis is confined to only the notes on which they are located; the other similar notes which follow are considered to be by themselves natural.

Concerning Nuances

In order to more accurately convey the varieties of nuances needed to faithfully render the meaning of the text we have found it necessary to adopt in psaltic notation Italian signs and terms of nuance. These signs and terms used in Western liniar notation are well known and are in almost universal usage.

Therefore we have adopted as terms of nuance: piano (p) - soft sweet; pianissimo (pp) - very soft; forte (f) - strong; mezzo-fort (mf) - stronger; and also crescendo (cresc. or $<$) and decrescdeno (decresc. or $>$).

Otherwise we should know that the melodic line itself largely indicates the nuances that necessarily must be applied in phrasing. For example, as the melodic line ascends, it should be sung more and more strongly; as it descends, more and more softly, that is crescendo and decrescendo.

THE DIATONIC SCALE AND MARTYRIA

The musical scale which we have used from the beginning of the book and with which we have sung the various exercises is called the <u>Diatonic Scale</u> because it is formed only by tones and semitones.

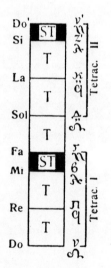

In as much as we have in psaltic music neither a staff nor keys which indicate to us the precise location of every note of the scale, there was a need for various symbols called martyria (indicators).

Martyria (indicators) are placed on each step of the scale and indicate, at the same time, the name of the step and the kind of scale (in the case before us--the Diatonic Scale).

Each step of the scales has a martyria which is composed of two symbols located one on top of the other. The symbol on top is the first initial of the name of the step (in Greek letters) and the symbol below indicates the type of scale. Analyzing the scale shown here, we see that the lower symbol of each martyria of the first tetracord is repeated in the same order in the second tetracord.

46

We should also notice that the martyria of the second tetracord are distinguished from those of the first by two commas (,,) underneath Di and Ke and by an apostrophe on Zo and high Ni ($.z'$ v').

<u>NOTE</u>: Exercise by reading and singing the diatonic scale, taking note of the martyria of each step.

THE DIATONIC SCALE AND ITS PHTHORAI

Along with the martyria, the diatonic scale also has for each step another symbol called a phthora. The phthorai peculiar to the diatonic scale

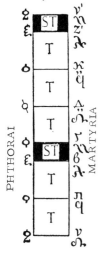

are called diatonic phthorai. And they also in many ways strengthen the scale as we will see more precisely when we learn other types of scales other than the diatonic.

There are eight diatonic phthorai called:
$\Omega = vi$; $Q = \eta a$; $\mathcal{E} = \beta u$; $Q = \gamma a$; $\mathbf{Q} = \Delta i$; $\delta = \kappa e$; $\mathcal{E} = z o$; $Q = vi$.

In the diatonic scale as here presented you can clearly see on the right side the diatonic martyria and on the left side the diatonic phthorai.

<u>NOTE</u>: The word phthora in Greek means to brake, or in the musical sense, to change or alter.

Concerning the Tones or Ihoi

In ecclesiastical music by tone or ihos we do not understand the tone or voice of a person, but rather a certain type of melody bound to a specific scale.

The Eastern Orthodox Church, in its ritual, uses eight tones arranged according to specific rules by St. John of Damascus in the 8th century. But the melodic origin of these tones dates much early, having its roots in the ancient popular music of Greece and Asia Minor, the part of the world that was the cradle of Christianity.

The Fathers taking into consideration the origin of the hymns, divided the tones of the church into <u>authentic</u> (or primitive) <u>tones</u> and <u>plagal</u> (derivative or related) <u>tones</u>.

The authentic are the I, II, III and IV tones. Taking into consideration the place of their origin they took on the following names:

Tone I - Dorian   Tone III - Phrygian

Tone II - Lydian   Tone IV - Milesian or Mixolydian

The plagal are the V, VI, VII and VIII tones derived from the four authenic tones. They take the following names from them:

Tone V - Hypodorian   Tone VII - Hypophrygian

Tone VI - Hypolydian   Tone VIII - Hypomilesian or Hypomixolydian

The ecclesiastical tones have been divided into three categories according to their scale or tonality:

I - Diatonic Tones: I, V, IV, VIII

II - Chromatic Tones: II, VI

III - Enharmonic Tones: III, VII

Each tone has a particular symbol, indicating a key, which is written at the beginning of the hymn in this way:

Tone I has the symbol 𝄞 and its plagal, Tone V, has the symbol ᵛ or ᵏ ᵛ

Tone II has the symbol ⏜ and its plagal, Tone VI, has the symbol ⏝ or ᵏ ⏝

Tone III has the symbol 𝄢. and its plagal, Tone VII, has the symbol ͞αͥ͞ or ᵏ ͞αͥ͞

Tone IV has the symbol 𝄞ͧ and its plagal, Tone VIII has the symbol οͥ. or ᵏ οͥ.

48

After the key signature it is customary to also add the name of the interval which is the base or vasis of the scale (the tonic of the tone). For example for Tone VIII: ὄλ. γι.

Melodic Formula. Before beginning to sing a piece of psaltic music, the ecclesiastical singer (psaltis) has the custom of formulating an impression (the tonality) of the tone of this piece through a melodic formula composed of a few of the characteristic notes which give an idea of the respective tone. These formulae will be indicated when studying each tone. In the ancient music these formulae were tied to mnemotechnic (rememberance) words. For example, for Tone I - Ananes, for Tone II - Neanes, etc. Today we no longer use similar designations, rather we simply sing the names (paralagi) of the notes of the formulae.

For example, here is the melodic formula for Tone VIII.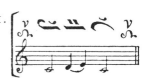

CONCERNING CADENCES

By cadence we understand the pause which is made in singing on the different steps of the scale. Cadences in music have the same function as punctuation in writing. There are four types:

1. Semicadence corresponds to a comma, and it is the pausing on the 5th step of the scale in which the hymn is written.

2. Imperfect Cadence is the pausing on the 3rd or other step (except for the 1st or 5th step). It corresponds in punctuation to a comma or often, depending upon the text, to a semicolon.

3.   Perfect Cadence is the pausing on the 1st step and corresponds

in punctuation to a semicolon or to a period, when it is found at

the end of a complete thought in the hymn.

4.   Final Cadence is the stop made on the 1st step at the end

of the hymn and always corresponds to the final period.

The cadences are indicated by their respective martyria and they also

have the function of facilitating the correct singing by paralagi (i.e.,

by the names of the notes).

OBSERVATIONS CONCERNING THE CADENCES AND RECITATIVE AND PAPADICA TEMPOS

The pauses produced by cadences on the different steps of the scales are

noted by a duration longer than one beat, that is having a temporal sign of

prolongation (clasma, apli, etc.) and being followed by the respective

martyria.

Here is an example of a semicadence in the VIII tone:

The cadences divide the singing into musical sentences and phrases.

We will see the rule for forming different cadences of each tone, according

to the tempo in which the hymn is written.   Through the assistance of the

cadences we are able to distinguish between two tone which use the same

scale and the same tonic (vasis).   For example Tones I and V, which use the

same diatonic scale and the same tonic (vasis) are distinguished by the

imperfect and final cadences as we will see later when studying these tones.

That which has been discussed above concerning cadences is applicable only to those hymns sung in the stihirarica and irmologica tempos because the recitative tempo does not in fact form cadences but is used only to recite the verses (stihi) which preceed the various hymns of Vespers and Matins, in the ison of the respective tone's tonic (vasis). Similarly, we will not encounter in our study of the tones the rules regulating the cadences for the papadica tempo.

As we saw in the chapter on tempos, the papdica tempo is used in hymns which are sung extremely slowly, i.e., Heruvika and Koinonkia. It is also used in some axions, polyeleoi, and other hymns which today are rarely encountered except in some monasteries and churches with an ancient monastic tradition.

The hymns of this tempo are not performed according to the cadence rules of the tones. The martyria, which usually mark the resolve of the cadences, in the singing of papadica hymns, serve only to guide the direction of the melody and is more often found on the tonic (vasis) of the tone and rarely on other steps.

The papadic hymn is a distinct genre of singing, a result of the freer inspiration of the psaltic composer.

THE DIATONIC TONES

Ecclesiastical hymns make use of eight tones or ihoi. Out of these four are diatonic: I, IV, V and VIII. They use the diatonic scale with which we are already familiar. We will begin our study of the tones with the first.

The First Tone (Dorian Ihos)

The first tone makes use of the diatonic scale with which we are familiar, but it begins on Pa (Re) its tonic or vasis. In singing, due to the law of the attraction of sounds, Zo almost always becomes flatted in descent (Ti flat).

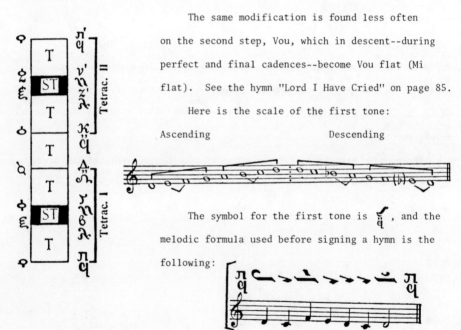

The same modification is found less often on the second step, Vou, which in descent--during perfect and final cadences--become Vou flat (Mi flat). See the hymn "Lord I Have Cried" on page 85.

Here is the scale of the first tone:

Ascending   Descending

The symbol for the first tone is ⌇ , and the melodic formula used before signing a hymn is the following:

In this tone, because we frequently meet Zo flat (Ti flat) we place it as a constituative element of the key signature.

Cadences of the First Tone

In the stihararica tempo, tone one has an imperfect cadence in GA (Fa) and Pa (Re); perfect and final in Pa (Re).

In the irmologic tempo, we find the imperfect cadence on Di (Sol); the perfect and final on Pa (Re).

Observations:

a) The usual scale of the first tone used in singing extends from Ni (Do) below Pa (Re) to Ke (La). In hymns which extend beyond this we find cadences on other steps than those discussed above.

b) The first kathisma and that "Glory," and "Now and Ever" which we encounter at Matins are sung according to the scales of the second tone, which we will discuss later.

This type of hymn is encounter having been written with the chromatic phthora ♏ ⟶of the second tone placed on the note Ke which takes the name Di and which causes Ke (La) to be flatted throughout the hymn. In order to make the execution of the hymn easier, we have placed this phthora on Di. This placement upon Di is much more suited to the execution of the hymn, both for the phthora and for the cadences as they are in fact found in the hymns of the second tone.

c) In the old system of psaltic music, the Dorian ihos had its own phthora called umanes (℺) placed, like we do today, on Ke, which serves as the vasis of this tone. It is preserved today, in the same form, in hymns called: Tone one-tetraphone.

EXAMPLE: of a Stihirarica . Hymn in Tone I

"Lord I Have Cried"   Tone I

Andante

O - Lord I have cried un-to Thee - - O, lis-

O - Lord I have cried un-to Thee - O, lis-

- ten to me; O lis-ten to me, O - -

- ten to - me O lis -ten to me- O - -

Lord!   O Lord I have cried un-to Thee O lis -ten -

Lord!   O Lord I have cried un-to Thee O lis-ten -

- to - me; give an ear to the voice of- - -

- to - me; give an ear to - -the voice of - -

my sup- pli-ca- - - tion when I -

my sup - pli-ca - - tion when I -

- call- up- - on - - - Thee - has-

— call - up- on - - - Thee - has-

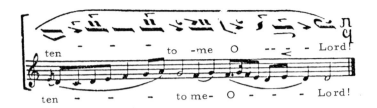

Observation: In order to clearly show the law of the attraction of sounds over Zo and Vou, we have used, both in psaltic and liniar notation, the respective accidentals.

EXAMPLE OF AN IRMOLIGCA HYMN IN TONE I

"O Thou who art the Joy of the Heavenly Hierarchs" (Prologue)

AN EXAMPLE OF AN IRMOLOGICA HYMN IN TONE I (in the form of Tone II)

"Thy Tomb O Savior" Kathisma

Tone I

după Macarie

Moderato

THE PLAGAL OF THE FIRST TONE OR FIFTH TONE (Hypodorian Ihos)

The plagal of the first or fifth tone uses the same diatonic scale as that of tone one.

It has two tonics or vasis:

In the stihirarica tempo its vasis is Pa (Re)

In the Irmologica tempo its vasis is Ke(La)

The symbol for the fifth tone is ꝗ, to which is added the name of the vasis or tonic: Pa (Re) or Ke(La). Example Tone V ꝗ ᴨᵢ or Tone V ꝗ ᴋe.

Here is the scale of the fifth tone with its tonic on Pa (Re)

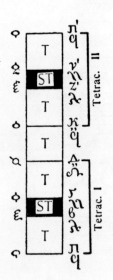

In order to enter the tone, Tone V uses two melodic formulae:

1) For the stihirarica tempo:

2) For the irmologica tempo:

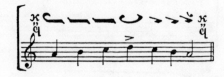

The key signature for tone five in the stihirarica tempo and for <u>Agem</u> is the following:

58

CADENCES OF THE PLAGAL OF THE FIRST OF FIFTH TONE

A)   In the stihiarica tempo Tone V has its semicadence on Ke(La); imperfect and perfect on Pa (Re) and final on Di(Sol) when there are more verses or stihi, and on Pa (Re) on the final verse or stih, that is the one with a "Glory" or a "Now and Ever."

B)   In the irmologica tempo we find the imperfect cadence on high Ni (High Do) and the perfect and final on Ke(La).

Observations:

1)   Tone V stihirarica uses the entire diatonic scale from Low Pa (Re) to High Pa (Re), causing, almost always, Zo(Ti) to be flatted while descending and less often Vou(Mi) to be flatted, due to the law of attraction of sounds.

2)   Tone V irmologica uses only the tetracord from Ke to Pa (La-Re) sometimes touching Di(Sol) below Ke(La), and Vou (Mi) above Pa (Re).

3)   Oftentimes, in the irmologica tempo, Ke has the phthora of Pa like this: $\underline{\text{o}\checkmark}$. This means that the tetracord Ke-Pa (La-Re) should be sung just like the first tetracord Pa-Di (Re-Sol) of the first tone.

4)   Another variant of this tone is the so-called: Tone V Agem, which has on Zo the agem (or enharmonic) phthora (♪) which causes this note to be flatted by a halftone both when descending and ascending, while the other notes remain unaffected maintaining their place on the diatonic scale. The cadences of the Fifth Tone Agem are: imperfect on Di, Zo, and Pa (Sol, Ti, and Re); perfect and final on Pa (Re). We find: doxologies, axions and liturgical responses written in this scale. When transcribing hymns of Tone V agem to liniar notation, Ti Flat, which corresponds to Zo Agem is written into the key signature in the same way as for hymns of the stihirarica tempo.

EXAMPLE OF A STIHIRARICA HYMN IN TONE V
"Lord I have Cried"

Tone V ҃ц ла ҃е.

when I - call up -on - - Thee has -

when I - - call up -on - - - Thee, has -

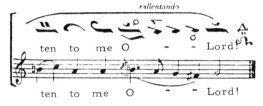

rallentando

ten to me O - - Lord!

ten to me O - - Lord!

EXAMPLE OF AN IRMOLOGICA HYMN IN TONE V (Ke like Pa)
"Isaiah Dance" (from the wedding service)

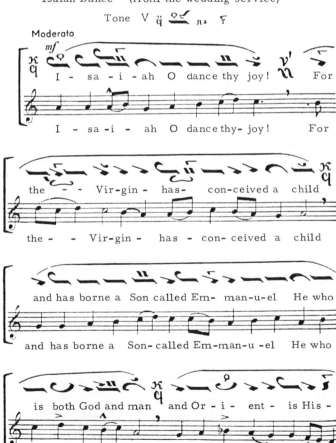

I - sa - i - ah O dance thy joy! For

I - sa - i - ah O dance thy- joy! For

the - - Vir-gin - has- con-ceived a child

the - - Vir-gin - has - con- ceived a child

and has borne a Son called Em- man-u-el He who

and has borne a Son- called Em-man-u -el He who

is both God and man and Or - i - ent - is His -

is both God and man and Or -i - ent- is His -

name. — and be-cause we magni—fy-Him

We can call the Vir-gin Bless-ed

AN EXAMPLE OF TONE V 'Agem' from the "Doxology"

Tone V

de A. PANN

Glo-ry be to Thee— who has shown us the

light — Glo-ry be to God in the

high-est and up-on the earth-- peace and

good-will a-mong all-- hu-man-kind!

THE FOURTH TONE (Milisian or Mixolydian Ihos)

The Fourth Tone makes use of the diatonic scale, except that its vasis (tonic) varies according to the tempo in which the hymn is written.

Therefore, in the papadica tempo the tonic is $\overset{A}{\underset{.}{..}}$ Di (Sol) (the natural tonic of the fourth tone), while in the stirirarica and irmologica tempos the tonic (vasis) is Vou(Mi).

Tone four in the irmologica tempo is also called legetos. Here is the scale of the fourth tone with all of its variants and branches.

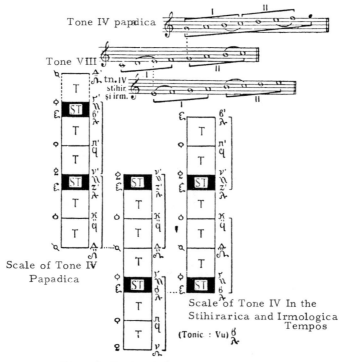

Tone IV papadica

Tone VIII

Scale of Tone IV
Papadica

Scale of Tone IV In the
Stihirarica and Irmologica
Tempos

(Tonic : Vu)

Diatonic Scale of Tone VIII
(Tonic : Ni)

Melodic Formulae of the Fourth Tone

In Papadica:

In Stihirarica:

In Irmologica:

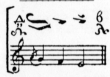

The symbol for the fourth tone is $\overset{\smile}{\underset{\sim}{\curlyvee}}$, to which is added the initial of the basis, for example, Tone $\overset{\smile}{\underset{\sim}{\curlyvee}}$ Bou.

This tone presents a number of difficulties in execution. In order to sing it correctly, you must remember that Zo(Ti) is at all times diatonic (natural). An exception to this rule is found in irmologica hymns legetos in which Zo(Ti)--because of the law of attraction of sounds--becomes flatted when descending. This Zo flat is also encountered when musical phrases tend towards a perfect cadence on Pa, that is when there is a phrase in the first or fifth tones, which have as a rule Zo flatted in descent.

Cadences of the Fourth Tone

In the stihirarica tempo, with the basis on Vou(Mi) tone four has the
following cadences: imperfect on Di(Sol) and Vou(Mi), perfect on Pa(Re);
and final on Vou(Mi).

The irmologica tempo called legetos with the vasis also on Vou(Mi)
has the following cadences: imperfect on Di, Vou and Pa (Sol, Mi, and Re)
and perfect and final in Vou(Mi).

With regard to the papadica tempo--as we said in a previous chapter--
these hymns do not in fact have cadences, but only martyria which indicate
the direction of the hymn, with only the martyria $\overset{\Lambda}{c\iota.}$ at the end of the hymn
taking the place of a final cadence.

NOTE 1: From the frequent perfect cadences in Pa, which we encounter
when singing the fourth tone, we must not come to the false conclusion that
this Pa could be thought of as a tonic (vasis) of a variant of this tone.
This cadence on Pa occurs only for variety and to avoid the use of Ni which
is a fundament of its sister tone--i.e., the eighth.

NOTE 2: In the apolitykia and kontakia of the fourth tone we will encounter
a new phthora called ⋏ᵢ = -ᶠ⁻ . It assumes the properties of the second
tone causing Ke(La) to be flatted throughout the hymn, in this way creating
a distance of a tone and a half between Ke(La) and Zo(Ti). We will become
better acquainted with this phthora when we study the scale of the second
tone.

EXAMPLE OF A STIHIRARICA HYMN OF TONE IV "Lord I Have Cried"

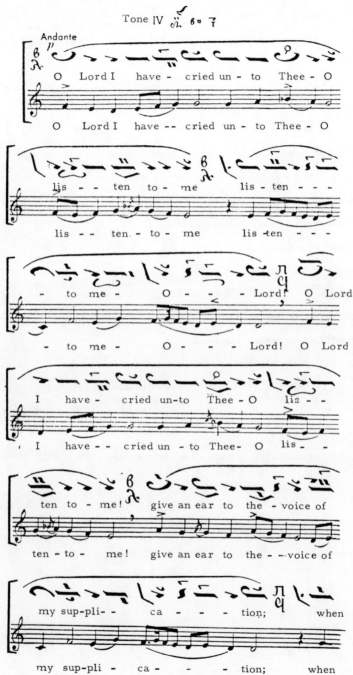

66

AMPLE OF AN IRMOLOGICA HYMN IN TONE IV-Legetos "From my youth" (Antiphon)

Tone IV

Note: Any accidental is effective only over the note on which it is placed. The effect is maintained in the case of a note which is immediately repeating the same sound. See the note Ti flat repeated in the third staff.

EXAMPLE OF A HYMN IN TONE IV (Apolytikion in the form of Tone II)
Apolytikion of Sts. Peter and Paul

Tone

de St. Popescu

Moderato

O ye who a-mong the A-pos-tles have filled

O ye who a-mong the A-pos-tles have filled

the first seats- in their ranks and are tea-chers of

the first seats- in their ranks and are tea-chers of

the whole world with the Mas-ter of all in-ter-ceed

the whole world with the Mas-ter of all in-ter-ceed

for-us that He might-give to the whole world-

for-us that He might-give to the whole world-

peace and that He might give our souls his great mer-

peace and that He might give our-souls his great mer-

- - cy -

- - cy -

THE PLAGAL OF THE FOURTH OR EIGHT TONE (Hypomixolydian Ihos)

This tone make use of the diatonic scale, having its tonic (vasis) on Ni(Do). It corresponds to the Do Major scale of Western/liniar music.

Here is the diatonic scale of the eighth tone and the Do Major scale, its equivalent, in Western/liniar music:

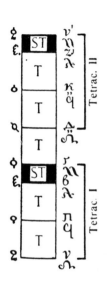

The symbol for the eighth tone is , and is melodic formula, the formula which has the same role as the arpeggio in western/liniar music, is the following:

The cadences of the eighth tone, which are the same both in the stihirarica and irmologica tempos, are the following:

Semicadence on the fifth step--Di(Sol); imperfect cadence on the third step--Vou(Mi), and a perfect and final cadence on the first step--Ni(Do).

NOTE 1: We will oftentimes find Zo(Ti) flatted in this tone. This Zo(Ti) flat is due to the law of attraction, of which we will speak later.

NOTE 2: Troparia, kontakia and kathismata, although they make use of the same scale, the tonic (vasis) in moved from Ni(Do) to Ga(Fa) with the help of the phthora of 𝑣ᵢ (⟶) placed on Ga giving birth to the scale called: Triphone Diatonic. In this case the imperfect cadence will be on Di(Sol) and the perfect and final cadences will be on Ga.

Here is the triphone diatonic scale of the eighth tone:

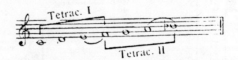

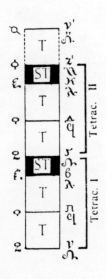

By these diagrams it can be clearly seen that the first tetracord Ni-Ga(Do-Fa) is exactly like the one of the preceeding scale of the eighth tone. When we sing higher up the scale--from Ga as though it were Ni(Fa as though it were Do) we must do the following. On Ga(Fa) we must place the phthora and the lower martyria of Ni(Do) from the first tetracords, in this way constructing the same tetracord above as you have below (tone, tone, semitone).

Similarly we will also place the phthora and lower martyria of Pa on Di; we will place the phthora and lower martyria of Vou on Ke; we will place the phthora and lower martyria of Ga on Zo, and we will place on high Ni the phthora of Di Ai (ˀα) but the martyria will be exactly as for lower Ni, but with an apostrophy (ʼᵥ).

NOTE: In the liniar transcription, Zo flat is translated by a flat in the key signature, thusly:

EXAMPLE OF A STIHIRARICA HYMN IN TONE VIII "Let my supplication"

TONE VIII öj. ri ř

...danie
p

Let my sup-pli- ca -tion be   set be-fore Thee

Let my sup-pli-ca- tion be set be- fore Thee

as the in -cense ris-ing be -   fore ——————

as the in -cense ris-ing be -   fore————

Thee   and the lift - ing up - of my -

Thee   and the lift - ing up - of my -

71

NOTE: Keeping in mind the fact that voices of singers vary (bass, baritone, tenor, etc.) pslatic hymns can be executed higher or lower according to the voice of the singer, without regard to the actual pitch of the scale in which the hymn is written.

AN EXAMPLE OF AN IRMOLOGICA HYMN IN TONE VIII
"What shall we call you?" (Prologue)

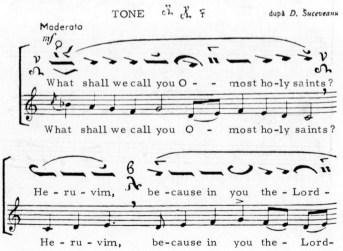

has tak - en rest; Se-ra- phim, be-cause in-

has tak - en rest; Se-ra-phim, be-cause in-

ces-sant-ly - you - glo- ri - fy Him;

ces-sant- ly - you - glo- ri - fy Him;

An - gels, be - cause you've o-ver- come flesh;

An - gels, be - cause you've- o- ver- come flesh;

The Pow- - -ers, be-cause you - - have - worked

The Pow - - - ers, be- cause you - - have - worked

mir-ac-les; Man - y are the names- which

mir - ac-les; Man - y are the names- which

we call you but more are the gifts you've giv-

en O pray for - us that the Lord may

save our souls- that He may save our souls.

EXAMPLE OF AN IRMOLOGICA HYMN IN TONE VIII
(The tempo for apolytikia, kontakia, etc.)
"God is the Lord"

God is - the Lord and - has re-vealed

God is - the Lord and - has re-vealed

Him-self - - to - - us   Bless-ed is - he

Him-self - - - to - - us   Bless-ed is - he

who comes in the name of the- Lord!

who comes in the name of- the- Lord!

THE SECOND TONE (Lydian Ihos)

The second tone uses its own chromatic scale, having its tonic (vasis) on Di(Sol) and less frequently on Vou and Ni(Mi and Do). Likewise, it has its own chromatic phthorai and martyria. The martyria are: ᴗ for Ni, Vou, Di, and Zo, and ♪ for Pa, Ga, Ke, and high Ni. The phthoria are: on Di which cause Ke(La) to be flatted and ♪ on Ke which cause Ke and Pa (La and Re) to be flated.

Here is the scale of the second tone:

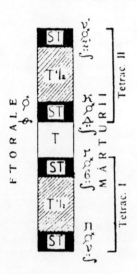

We can see that this scale is composed of two identical tetrachords separated by the distance of a whole tone.

The center of the scale is its tonic Di(Sol). The note which is continually heard throughout hymns written in this tone.

The symbol for the second tone is ᴗ͞ and the melodic formula is the following:

The Key Signature: In this tone, because the sixth step, Ke(La), is continually flat throughout, in transcription we use the following key signature:*

---

*) We have not introduced Pa flat of the first tetracord into the key signature in transcription because this tetracord is rarely used, the melody usually descending only as far as Vou(Mi).

Cadences of the Second Tone

1.   In the stihirarica Tempo: imperfect cadences on Di, Vou, and
Zo (Sol, Mi, and Ti) and sometimes on Low Ni (Do); perfect cadences on
Di and Vou (Sol, Mi) and final on Di (Sol).

2.   In the irmologica tempo, which make use of two variant scales,
we have the following cadences:

a)   In hymns written using the scale of the second tone: imperfect
cadences on Di (Sol); perfect on Vou (Mi) and final on Di (Sol).
This form is used for: apolytikia (Troparia of the day); kathismata;
as well as other hymns suited to the scale of the second tone.

b)   In hymns which use the scale borrowed from the Sixth Tone (which,
as we will see, is an elaboration of the scale of the second tone,
except for a single difference--that it begins on Pa instead of Ni)
we have the following cadences: imperfect on Di (Sol) and perfect
on final on Pa (Re).

This form is used for: Aposticha; Antiphones; The Beatitudes
as well as other hymns suited to the scale of the sixth tone.

give an ear to the - - voice of - my sup-

give an ear to the - - voice of - - my sup-

pli - ca - - tion, when I —

pli - ca - - tion, when I - -

call - up - on - - - Thee has - ten - -

call - up - on - - - Thee has - ten - -

- - to - - me - - O - Lord-

- - to - - - me - - O - - -Lord-

EXAMPLE OF AN IRMOLOGICA HYMN IN TONE II (The form proper to Tone II)
"When Thou did descend" (The Apolytikion of the Resurrection)

did res-ur -rect those dead from the low-er re-

did res-ur --rect those dead from the low-er re-

gions then all the hea-ven-ly pow-

gions then all the hea-ven-ly pow-

ers - cried a-loud O Thou Who art the

ers - cried a-loud O Thou Who art the

Giv-er of life O Christ Thou who

Giv-er of-Life O Christ Thou Who

art o-ur God - - glo-ry be

art o-ur God - - glo-ry be

to - - Thee

to - - - Thee!

EXAMPLE OF AN IRMOLOGICA HYMN IN TONE II (Form of Tone VI)
"Thy Holy Resurrection" (Aposticha)

*) In singing this hymn according to the psaltic notation, we must take note of the phthora ➷ ꓕ of the sixth tone which cause Vou and Zo (MI-Sol) to be flatted and Ga and high Ni (Fa and high Do) to be sharped.

Note: In order that you might become thoroughly acquainted with the sound and structure of the sixth tone, we have placed the accidentals in the course of the liniar music rather than in the key signature.

THE PLAGAL OF THE SECOND TONE, THE SIXTH TONE (Hypolydian Ihos)

The plagal of the second tone makes use of two scales, namely:
a) the chromatic scale proper to the sixth tone, with the vasis (tonic)
on Pa (Re) having its own particular martyria and phthorai; and b)
the chromatic scale of the second tone which, as we know, has its tonic
on Di (Sol).

Here is the chromatic scale proper to the plagal of the second tone:

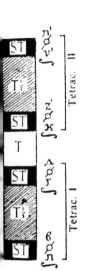

This scale has two similar chromatic
tetracords constructed with the assistance of its
two phthora ♪ and ♦ , which causes Vou and
Zo (Mi and Ti) to be flatted and Ga and high Ni
(Fa and high Do) to be sharped.

It has the following chromatic martyria:

The symbol for the sixth tone is ♫ ⌣, and
its melodic formula is:

Key Signature

The accidentals which form the key signature, have effect only over
those notes which comprise the octave used, i.e., Pa-Pa (Re-Re).

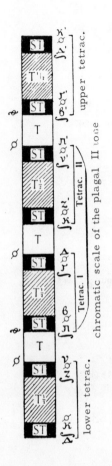

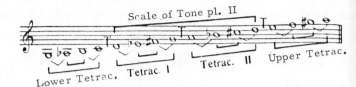

There are hymns which go beyond the limits of the octave, going above high Pa (Re) and going below low Pa (Re). You can see that these instances produce great modifications in singing some of the notes.

This diagram of the chromatic scale of the sixth tone shows the extensions above and below the octave.

In carefully analyzing the two tetracords which extend the scale above and below, we see that in the extention, the steps of the scale undergo modifications with the exception of Di (Sol) of the tetracord below the scale and of Ke (La) of the tetracord above the scale.

NOTE: The extentions of the octave, above and below, are rarely encountered, and only in papadica or stihirarica hymns of the sixth tone.

The Cadences of the Sixth Tone

In the stihirarica tempo we have: a semicadence on Ke (La), imperfect cadence on Di (Sol), and perfect and final cadences on Pa (Re).

The irmologica tempo makes use of two scales:

a)   The scale proper to the sixth tone, in which the verses of the Vesper's psalm, doxologies, and other hymns are sung. The cadences are: imperfect on Di (Sol) and perfect and final on Pa (Re).

b)   The scale of the second tone, in which the apolitykia (troparia of the day) kathismata, and other hymns are sung. The cadences are: imperfect on Di (Sol), and perfect and final on Vou (Mi).

NOTE: In many hymns we encounter a mixed scale of the sixth tone: a) with the first tetracord chromatic and the second diatonic; b) with the first tetracord diatonic and the second chromatic.

Here is how they are diagramed:

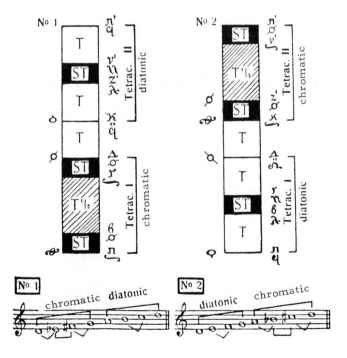

85

EXAMPLE OF A STIHIRARICA HYMN IN TONE VI "Lord I have Cried"

EXAMPLE OF AN IRMOLOGICA HYMN (Form of Tone VI) In TONE VI
From the "Doxology"

Tone VI

de ȘTEFANACHE POPESCU

Glo - ry be to Thee - who has shown to us the

Glo-ry be to Thee - who has shown to us the

light -   Glo- ry be un - to God in the high-est

light -   Glo - ry be un-to   God in the high-est

and   up -on   the earth peace   and good-will- a -

and   up -on   the earth- peace   and good-will- a -

mong - all hu-man - - kind!

mong - all hu-man - - - kind!

EXAMPLE OF AN IRMOLOGIC HYMN IN TONE VI (Form of Tone II)
"The Angelic Powers" (Apolytikion of the Resurrection)

Tone VI

după MACARIE

The An - - gel -ic pow-ers were- up - on Thy

The An- - gel -ic pow -ers were- up -on Thy

tomb   and those that watched- Thee were as dead   and

tomb   and those that watched Thee were as dead   and

Mar - - - y   stood -   at   the   tomb   look - ing

Mar - - - y   stood -   at   the   tomb   look - ing

for - - -   Thy most pre-cious bod -y   but

for _____   Thy most pre-cious bod-y   but

Thou has des- - -   - poiled   had -es   with - -

Thou has des- - -   - poiled   had-es   with - - -

- out be - ing tried by   him.   Thou has come

- out be - ing tried by   him.   Thou has come

down to meet____   the   Vir-gin   and   thus

down to meet____   the   Vir-gin   and   thus

grant _____   ing   life -   Thou who has a-

grant _____   ing   life -   Thou who has a-

89

NOTE: In general, the chromatic tones, i.e., the second and sixth, in irmologica hymns borrow the melodic formulae of each other's respective scales, for a greater degree of variety. Here is what Anton Pann says in this regard: "Those who structured ecclesiastical music have used the melodies of these two chromatic tones in this way, desiring to color the melody, so that it would not be monotonous: in the rapid-irmologica hymns of the second tone they used the scale of the plagal of the second (that is the sixth tone); and in rapid-irmologica melodies of the plagal of the second (that is the sixth tone) they used the scale of the second tone--and having created the practice, it has continued to be sung in this way until today." (Bazul Teoritic si Practic, pp. 105-106.)

In order to more clearly illustrate the interweaving of these two tones mentioned above, we offer an example from the typicon: the "Katavasia of Epiphany" by Anton Pann: The First Irmos ("In the Depths of the Sea") and the second irmos ("Verily Israel") both written in the irmologica tempo. The impression that is given when moving from one irmos to the other is most powerful, most beautiful and very majestic.

FROM THE KATAVASIA OF EPIPHANY "Having Uncovered the Bottom"

Irmologica Hymn Tone II

(in the form of Tone VI)

A. PANN

FROM THE KATAVASIA OF EPIPHANY   "Verily Israel"

Irmologica Hymn Tone VI Pl. II from C tone II T

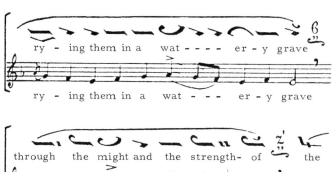

ry - ing them in a wat - - - - er - y grave

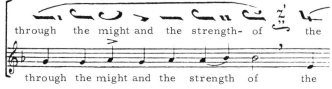

through the might and the strength of the

right - hand of our Mas-ter.

THE THIRD TONE (Phrygian Ihos)

The third tone makes use of the diatonic scale, improperly called by some enharmonic. Enharmonic, in psaltic music, is nothing more than Zo (Ti) being lower close to Ke (La) and Vou (Mi) being raised closer to Ga (Fa) through the assistance of the phthora ♪ called <u>agem</u>, the phthora of the third and seventh tones.

Here is the scale of the third tone:

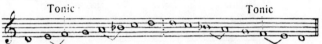

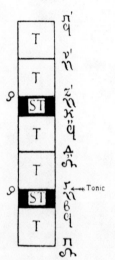

NOTE I: This scale, although it begins on Pa (Re), has as its vasis (tonic) on Ga (Fa), which is at the center of the scale. In the course of singing hymns, we find that the scale descends to low Ni (Do).

NOTE II: The melodic line of this tone is very similar to that of Tones I and V and only at the end in the final moments, as it goes into the final cadence in Ga (Fa) does it give the impression of Fa major.

NOTE III: Inasmuch as the third tone borrows, in the composition of its hymns, the melodic formulae of Tones I and V, that is notes Zo (Ti) and Vou (Mi) variable, the phthora ♪ (agem) does not have a permanent character in this tone, but those two notes, are subject to the law of the attraction of sounds, and are executed as though Zo (Ti) had a simple flat on it, and the distance between Vou-Ga (Mi-Fa) with the interval of a semitone as in the diatonic scale.

NOTE IV: The verse of the Vespers Psalm and of the Matins Praises are sung in the irmologica tempo. "Lord I Have Cried" and "Glory and Now" are sung in the stihirarica tempo, that is more slowly, render in liniar music by the term "Andatino."

The symbol for the third tone is 𝑖𝑖 to which is added the name of its vasis (tonic), *ya*, in this way: Tone III, 𝑖𝑖 *ra.* . When the following is also added to the symbol: Tone III 𝑖𝑖 ⌐◠ 𝑑𝑙 it means that we begin from Pa (Re), the note on which the preceeding hymn or verse ended.

Cadences (In the stihirarica and irmologica tempos)

 Imperfect: on Ke (La);

 Perfect: on Pa (Re) and sometimes on low Ni (Do);

 Final: on Ga (Fa).

Here is the melodic formula of the third tone with its key signature (Ti flat):

NOTE: The diatonic scale of the third tone, for the papadic tempo, is formed with the assistance of the diatonic phthora 𝑣𝑖 = 𝒬 place on Ga, it being sung as though it were from Ni (Do) of the diatonic scale. The symbol for this tone is: Tone III 𝑖𝑖 𝒬 𝑣𝑖. The cherubim and communion hymns are written in this scale, which being papadica have no rules with regard to cadences.

Tonelll ῆ va T

după NEAGU IONESCU

O - - - Lord I have cried un - to Thee -

O - - - lis - ten - to me - , Lis - ten - to

me O - - - Lord! O Lord I have

cried un -to Thee - O lis -ten - to me,

give - an ear to the - - voice of my

sup - pli - ca - - - - tion when I

- call up-on - - - - - Thee Has-

ten - - - to me O - - - Lord!

EXAMPLE OF AN IRMOLOGICA HYMN IN TONE III
"Let the Heavens Rejoice" (Apolytikion of the Resurrection)

Tone III ηͭ ra T̄

Din Liturghia Psaltică *de I. CROITORU*

Let all those in hea-ven be- - -come joy-ful

and be-come glad - all those dwell-ing on the earth

be-cause the Lord has been vic - tor-ious with his

migh-ty arm by trampl-ing down death - by -

His death He has be-come the first born from
His death He has be-come the first born from

the dead and through this He has res-cued us
the dead. and through this He has res-cued us

from - the -- bow-els of Hell and thus giv-
from - the - bow-els of Hell and thus giv-

ing the world great mer - - - - cy.
ing the world great mer - - - cy.

EXAMPLE OF A PAPADICA HYMN IN TONE III (On the diatonic scale)
A selection from the "Cherubim Hymn"

Tone III

de ȘTEFANACHE POPESCU

Note: From this example, it can be seen that in papadic hymns of this

tone, rules of cadence do not exist. This fact also applies to Communion

Hymns written in this scale.

100

THE SEVENTH TONE

Hymns written in the seventh tone make use of two forms of the scale, namely:

a)   The Enharmonic-Agem Form, which uses the enharmonic-agem scale, with the vasis (tonic) on Ga (Fa), and with the help of the agem phthora located on Zo and Ga. In order to distinguish this tone from the third the agem phthora located on Zo (Ti) has a permanent character throughout the course of the hymns. Regarding the agem on Ga, this does not have any effect; the Ga-Vou (Fa-Mi) interval being executed as diatonic in the same manner as in the third tone.

b)   The Diatonic Form, having its vasis (tonic) on low Zo (Ti). This form is called Varys or Proto-varys.

Here is the enharmonic-agem scale with the vasis on Ga (Fa):

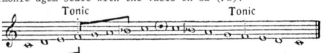

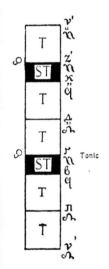

The enharmonic-agem scale of the seventh tone is identical with the Fa Major scale which has a Flat on Ti (Zo ♭'). Although it begins with Ni (Do), it has its vasis (tonic) on Ga (Fa). From the hymns written in this tone it can be observed that they mostly uses the two tetracords bound together by the tonic, that is Ni-Ga (Do-Fa) and Ga-Zo (Fa-Ti flat). The melodies go up to high Ni (Do) and often touch even Pa (Re). The symbol for the seventh tone is $\overline{\text{αγ}}$ or simply αγ .

Here is the melodic formula and the key signature:

101

Cadences

In both the stihirarica and irmologica tempos, the hymns written in this enharmonic-agem scale of the seventh tone have imperfect cadences on Di (Sol) and sometimes on Pa (Re); and perfect and final on Ga (Fa).

NOTE I: Sometimes a perfect cadences is also formed on low Ni when the sense of the text requires it.

NOTE II: The great majority of hymns in the seventh tone use this enharmonic-agem scale with the vasis (tonic) on Ga (Fa).

The Varys and Proto-varys Diatonic Forms

There are two forms of Varys Diatonic. The first is Varys Diatonic proper and the second is a mixture of the first tone (protos) and Varys Diatonic called: Proto-varys.

Here is the scale of the Varys Diatonic form:

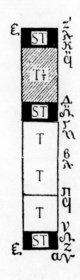

As we can see the scale used by the Varys Diatonic form is a diatonic scale with its vasis (tonic) on low Zo (Ti) natural. The name varys comes from the fact that this form has as its base note that most grave (the lowest) of all the tones, namely low Zo (Ti). The symbol for this form of the seventh tone is $\overrightarrow{a_{\gamma}}\ z\ o$, or simply $^{z\ o}_{a_{\gamma}}$ and its melodic formula is:

As you can see Ga (Fa) and Ke (La) are permanently sharped in this scale. Cadences are: imperfect on Ga and Di (Fa and Sol); perfect on Pa and low Zo (Re and low Ti); and a final cadence on low Zo (Ti).

The Proto-Varys Diatonic Form

The second form of Varys Diatonic is called Proto-Varys because, as stated above, it is a mixture of both the first and varys tones.

Here is the scale of this form:

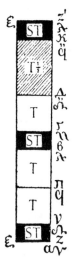

It makes use of the same symbols as for the Varys Diatonic above. The distinction comes in its use of the cadences borrowed from the Diatonic Tones I and V. We find imperfect cadences on Ga and Di (Fa and Sol)--found also in Tones I and V--as well as on high Zo (Ti); and perfect cadences on Pa (Re)--as in the first tone--and on low Zo (Ti); and final cadences on low Zo (Ti).

The melodic formula for this form is:

There is a third form of the seventh tone called Varys Enharmonic from high Zo ,Ϙ , which is not discussed in this work, and is rarely encountered.

EXAMPLE OF A STIHIRARICA HYMN IN TONE VII (Enharmonic form)
"Lord I have Cried"

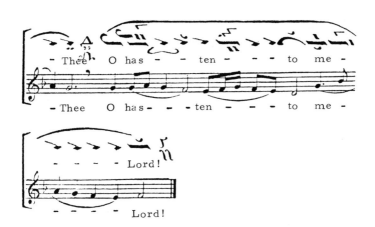

EXAMPLE OF AN IRMOLOGICA HYMN OF TONE VII
"Having destroyed death by Thy Cross" (Apolytikion of the Resurrection)

Tone VII

Din Liturghia Psaltică
de I. CROITORU

Moderato

mf

Hav-ing des-troyed death - by Thy Cross Thou has o- -

Hav-ing des-troyed death- by Thy Cross Thou has o--

pened Pa-ri- -dise to the - thief Thou has changed the

pened Pa-ri- -dise to the - - -thief Thou has changed the

lam-ent of the myrh-bear-ers to joy and Thou has com-

lam-ent of the myrh-bear-ers to joy and Thou has com-

mand-ed them to pro-claim un -to the A-post-les that Thou

mand-ed them to pro-claim un-to the A-post-les that Thou

has a - ris- en O Christ o-ur Lord and God grant-ing the

has a- ris -en O Christ o-ur Lord and God grant-ing the

- world- great- mer - - - cy.

- world- great- mer - - - cy.

EXAMPLE OF A HYMN IN TONE VII PROTO-VARYS
"In the Depths of the Sea" (Katavasia of Pentecost)

Tone VII

de ANTON PANN

Allegretto

In the depths - of the sea He - covered o - ver both the Phar- oah - - - and his Char - - i - ots He who with His migh-ty arm is a - ble to crush- war - fare Let us sing to Him for He - - has been - glo - ri -fied

Other Scales Formed Through the Help of the Phthorai: Zygos (), Cliton (⊘)
and Spathi ⊖⊢⊣

The Chromatic Phthora Zygos ⌇ and its Scale

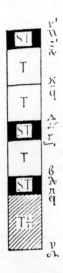

In addition to the chromatic phthorai of the
second tone (Di ⟶ and ϰe ⟶) and of the sixth tone
ϰa ⟶ şi ⅄i ⌇, we encounter another phthora ⌇ called
Zygos, which is located on Di (Sol) and causes
Pa and Ga (Re and Fa) to be sharped; the other
intervals remain diatonic.

The chromatic scale Zygos, formed with the
assistance of the Zygos phthora, is nothing more
than the diatonic scale of Tone VIII (Do Major) with
its second and fourth intervals modified upwardly,
causing it to become chromatic.

The chromatic scale Zygos is not found used in
its totality, but only in fragments, as is shown in
the example below taken from the "Katavasier" of
A. Pann.

108

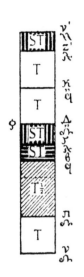

In the enharmonic family, in addition to the phthora agem (✿) which we know from Tones III and VII, we meet another phthora ✿ called Cliton which is placed on Di (Sol) and causes both Ga and Vou (Fa and Mi) to be sharped; the other intervals remain diatonic.

The enharmonic scale Cliton, formed with the assistance of the phthora Cliton, is nothing more than the diatonic scale of Tone VIII (Do Major) with its third and fourth intervals modified up-wardly: Vou and Ga (Mi and Fa) sharped.

In practice the enharmonic scale Cliton is not sung in its totality but only in fragments, as can be seen in the example below taken from "The Paraclisis Hymn."

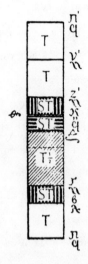

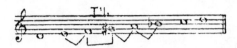

Another enharmonic phthora, which we meet in ecclesiastical music, is the phthora called Spathi which is placed on Ke (La) and causes Zo (Ti) to be flatted and Di (Sol) to be sharped; the other intervals remain diatonic.

The enharmonic scale Spathi, formed with the assistance of the Spathi phthora, is nothing more than the diatonic scale of Tones I and V with a vasis on Pa (Re), which has its fourth interval Di (Sol) sharped, and its sixth interval Zo (Ti) flatted.

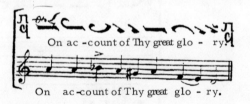

On ac-count of Thy great glo - ry.

On ac-count of Thy great glo - ry.

The Theory of the Law of the Attraction of Sounds

We have seen that in the first and fifth tones the intervals Vou and Zo are, in ascent, diatonic (i.e., natural). However, in descent, Zo (most often) and Vou (less often) are attracted to the steps immediately below, therefore they descend an additional semi-tone.

The tendency for these two steps to draw near to the step immediately above when ascending, and to the step immediately below when descending is produced by an accustical rule called the "Law of the Attraction of Sounds."

In keeping with these rules, each step within a scale fulfills a particular function, being bound and influenced by the vasis (tonic). Because of the way in which psaltic music borrows melodic formulae and cadences from one tone to another, it is natural that the influence of this law of the attraction of sounds would make itself very much felt.

Through this law the key to many of the enigmas involved in executing psaltic music is found. Through it one is able to create the specific atmosphere of this music, and also through it one is able to clearly explain all the questions and confusion involved in the problem of quarter tones. Similarly, through this law one can explain the affinity between some tones as well as the variences caused because of the different tempos.

And because in liniar notation each effect of the law of the attraction of sounds is shown and fixed by the respective accidentals, we have decided to also place, in the psaltic music, the effects of this law by placing the respective accidentals on the effected notes. In this way we hope to eliminate all confusion which often occurs today, causing mistakes in the execusion of psaltic music.

So that you might better understand what we have said above, regarding the precise placement of the effects of the law of attraction of sounds, we give you these fragments from the hymn: "Lord, I Have Cried," both in Tone I and Tone V:

Tone I

Tone Pl. I

112

We have seen that many times in Tone VIII when descending Zo (Ti) becomes Flat, because of the law of attraction, thus forming a major scale, without a 'note sensibile' (i.e., without there being a semitone between the 7-8 steps, i.e., a semi-tone before the tonic), a scale which has a unique musical quality. We give as an example the hymn "Blessed be the Name of the Lord" by Anton Pann in the Eighth Tone.

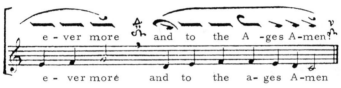

The Fourth Tone, which in fact has the same scale as the Eighth Tone, applies the law of attraction on the same step--Zo, descending by a semi-tone to Zo (Ti) flat. This is made permanent in the irmologica (legetos) tempo, with a final cadence in Vou (Mi), its vasis. We give as an example the irmos "I Shall Open My Mouth" by the Proto-Psaltes Emanoil Smeu and Neagu Ionescu.

113

The Third Tone, as we have already shown, has an affinity with Tones I and V. It makes use of the cadences of these tones and just in the last moments of the hymn, turns toward its final cadence in Ga, its feature (Fa Major). It is natural, therefore, that in singing one would apply to this tone the law of attraction in conjunction with the interweaving of the melody of the other two tones: I and V, although taking into account the change in tonics. This point can be seen clearly in the hymn "Let the Heavens Rejoice" in the Third Tone on page 97

The Seventh Tone enharmonic is very similar to the eighth tone from Ga (as though it were Ni) (Fa like Do). Evidence of this similarity can be seen in how the law of attraction is applied in this tone. For example, we have transposed the same hymn "The Wealthy Have Become Poor" into three tones:

Tone VIII ᵒᵏ F

We now transpose this same hymn, again in the Eighth Tone, but a fourth higher, that is in Fa Major, and we sing it exactly the same, on Ga as from Ni:

Tone

The weal-thy have be-come poor and be-come hun-

gry, but those who are search-ing for the - Lord -

- - will - not be in want - for that

which - is - good.

And if we write the same hymn once more with the martyria of the Seventh Tone enharmonic, and sing it, we realize that they sound exactly the same. This shows us that in reality, the Seventh Tone can be thought of as a diatonic tone:

In conclusion, if the Seventh Tone is exactly like the Eighth Tone from Ga as from Ni, it means that it is under the influence of the law of the attraction of sounds, as in the Eighth Tone, through the lowering of Zo by a semi-tone: i.e., Zo (Ti) flat.

In this way the Agem ♪ , which theoretically speaking takes an interval of less than a semi-tone, in contrast, works diatonically, its scale being one and the same as that of tone eight diatonic "Ga as from Ni." In order that we might dispell all the controversy around the model structure of this enharmonic-agem scale of the Seventh Tone, we give as an additional example a verse from the third stasis of the "Lamentations."

Tone VII Ga

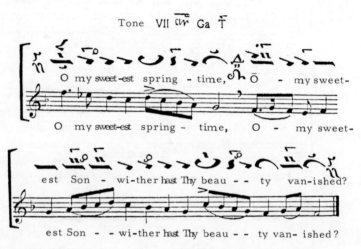

The second form of the scale of the Seventh Tone is the "Proto-varys" which has nothing in common with the first form, the so-called enharmonic.

In reality this proto-varys is a melodic formula whose range simply comprises a fifth, descending from Ga to Zo (Fa to Ti natural) its vasis (tonic) being low Di (Sol).

From the following four examples we can see that the note Ga (Fa), which begins the formula for proto-varys, is also common to Tones I and V. Ga, likewise, is a common note and fundamental to Tone Three, which as we know, has an affinity with the two tones mentioned above. And lastly, Ga is also common with and fundamental to Tone Seven.

a) Entrance into proto-varys from Tone I

b) Entrance into proto-varys from Plagal of Tone I

c) Entrance into protovarys from Tone III

d) Entrance into protovarys from Tone VII-enharmonic.

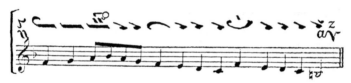

From the above examples, we can see that the proto-varys formula is obtained by a melodic mixture of Tones I, V, and III, the tones which, by the law of attraction have Zo diatonic (Ti natural) in ascent, and Zo (Ti) flat in descent. Zo (Ti) flat in descent, in Tones I, V, and III, forms with the note Ga (Fa) a perfect descending fourth: (Zo flat-Ga; Ti flat-Fa). Therefore one is assured of having the note Ga (Fa) well fixed in order to begin the formula of proto-varys.

What especially attracts our attention, however, is, that Zo (Ti) flat naturally and indestructably bound to Ga (Fa)--in the final cadence of the lower octave becomes Zo diatonic (Ti natural).

This shows us clearly that "Zo diatonic" (Ti natural) of the final cadence, is the third of the melody. Its true vasis, that is its fundament, is low Di (Sol), which, from the harmonic point of view, is able to form an interval equally consonant with "Zo diatonic (Ti natural)" and "Zo (Ti) flat."

The following two examples will show us more clearly the instance when "Zo diatonic" (Ti natural) could be considered as the vasis (tonic), as well as other aspects of the proto-varys form.

FROM THE PROTOVARYS DOXOLOGY

Tone VII $\overline{\alpha\gamma}$ z o

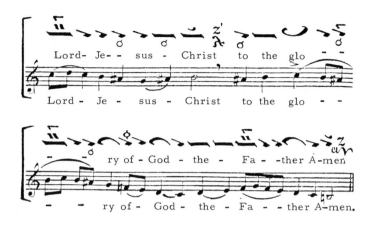

Lord- Je- - sus - Christ to the glo - -

Lord - Je - sus - Christ to the glo - -

ry of - God - the - Fa - -ther A-men

ry of - God - the - Fa - - ther A-men.

From these two examples it can be clearly seen that if, in this proto-varys form, the melodic range goes beyond Ga (Fa)--the note which begins the formula for proto-varys in descent--and especially if this melody hovers around Zo diatonic (Ti natural), then Ke and Ga (La and Fa) are altered upward, that is they become sharped. But if the melody returns, descending toward low Zo (Ti natural), Ga again becomes diatonic (Fa natural).

In other words, this scale which extends from low Zo (Ti natural) to high Zo (Ti natural), in ascent causes Ga and Ke (Fa and La) to be sharped, and when it descends, Ga becomes diatonic (Fa natural).

Example:

GENERAL CONSIDERATIONS ABOUT MARTYRIA AND PHTHORAI

From what we have learned up until now, we realize that psaltic musical notation has no other means than the signs called <u>Martyria and Phthorai</u> to demonstrate the melodic construction and the type of scale of a given hymn.

The Martyria

From their very name we know that the martyria are signs which "confess," that is show or confirm that at a given moment in a hymn we are on a specific note of the scale. Therefore they have the same role as keys and staffs in western liniar music.

In addition, they also indicate the cadences as well as the type of scale on which we are singing. For this reason they are composed of two parts, one on top of the other, each having its special significance.

Accordingly, the top sign of a martyria is the Greek initial of the name of the note from which we start or to which we have come in the course of the hymn. The bottom sign tells us in which scale the hymn is written (Diatonic, chromatic of enharmonic).

For example: $\mathcal{L}$. The letter ν , from the top part tells us that the name of the step with which we begin is Ni, but the bottom sign α tells us that we are in the diatonic scale.

Therefore, there must necessarily be three types of martyria: diatonic martyria, chromatic martyria, and enharmonic martyria.

But since the enharmonic scale uses as martyria the same symbols
as the diatonic scale, we actually have only two types of martyria--diatonic
and chromatic.

NOTES:

The martyria are often written at the beginning of a hymn in order to
indicate the type of scale and to serve as a point of departure for starting
the hymn. Therefore, usually at the beginning of a hymn, only the symbol
of the tone is written as we have seen in each hymn, it having the same
role as a key signature in western music. After that comes the name of the
note which is the vasis of the tone, and at the end the tempo in which the
hymn is sung is indicated.

Example   ολ. ν‹ 7̅

Here are the martyria of the diatonic and chromatic scales:

Diatonic Martyria: άγ. ολ. ϙ. Χ. η. ολ. η. Χ. Χ.

Chromatic Martyria {
of Tone II: ν. η. δ. ς. Δ. χ. ζ. ν.
of Tone IV: η. δ. ς. δ. Δ. δ. δ. η.
}

The martyria of the enharmonic scale are the same as the diatonic,
which are borrowed by the respective enharmonic scales (Agem, Spathi and
Cliton).

The Phthorai

In the chapter "The Diatonic Scale and the Diatonic Phthorai" we saw
that the name Phthora comes from the Greek; it means to alter or change, in
the sense that the intervension of a phthora placed on any note causes an
immediate change of scale in which you had been singing up until then, moving
to another scale. This operation is called modulation. We will speak of
modulation more completely in the following chapter.

The power of a phthora to change in a moment and unexpectedly the course of a hymn creates the beauty and charm of ecclesiastical psaltic music. This means that a single phthora has the power of an entire key signature in western music.

There are 18 phthorai in all and they are divided into three categories: diatonic, chromatic, and enharmonic.

There are eight diatonic phthorai, each step of the scale having its own.

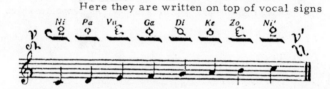

NOTE: The diatonic phthorai can be placed on other steps of the scale. A phthora placed on a step other than its own causes that note to lose its name, and that note takes the name and tonality of the phthora which has been placed on it.

For example:

Explanation: The sound represented by ⚬ is the same as the note before it, but because of the diatonic phthora of Ke ♂, it takes the name Ke and the following notes are named and sung as a diatonic fragment from Ke to low Pa.

124

Di (Sol)--The last note of the melodic fragment of the sixth

Tone (Chromatic) is an enharmonic sound (in the western music understanding)

with Ke (La double flatted) as a result of the diatonic phthora of Ke (**ο**).

In order to make this clearer, the transcription of the second

fragment, the diatonic, could be written in this manner:

However, when a phthora is located on is proper note, that is the

note which it represents, then this note retains its name, simply changing

the intonation according to the effect produced by the new phthora.

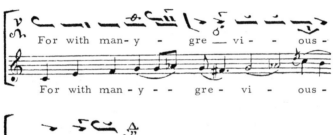

The Chromatic Phthorai: There are 5 chromatic phthorai, namely:

a)   Those of the Second Tone: The phthora of Di **-ο-** which may also

be written on Ni, Vou, and Zo, and the phthora of Ke- **♯** , which may also be

written on Pa, Ga, and Ni (look at the chromatic scale of second tone on

page 87).

NOTE: Both of the phthorai (Di- ⟨symbol⟩ and Ke- ⟨symbol⟩) can also be placed on any other note. In this case that note takes the name and intonation of the phthora placed on it; also the initial of the note to which we will be moving should also be written. (Ex. ⟨symbol⟩ or ⟨symbol⟩).

    b)   Those of the plagal of the second tone: The phthora proper to PA- ⟨symbol⟩ which is placed on low Pa, also on Ga, Ke, and high Ni ; and the phthora of Di- ⟨symbol⟩ which is also placed on low Ni, Vou, Zo and high Pa .

    c)   The Zygos phthora ⟨symbol⟩ which is place on Di and causes Pa and Ga to be sharped.

The Enharmonic Phthorai: There are a total of 5 enharmonic phthorai, namely:

    1)   Agem - ⟨symbol⟩ which is written on Zo, Vou, and Ga

    2)   Cliton - ⟨symbol⟩ which is written on Di

    3)   Spathi - ⟨symbol⟩ which is written on Ke

    4)   General Flat - ⟨symbol⟩ which is usually written on Ke and makes all the Zo's met within a given hymn flat until another change of phthora.

    5)   A General Sharp - ⟨symbol⟩ which is written on Ga and makes all Vou's met within a given hymn sharp.

NOTE: These two phthorai (general flat ⟨symbol⟩ and general sharp ⟨symbol⟩) are encounter very rarely in ecclesiastical music. The phthora ⟨symbol⟩ (general flat) often takes the place of the phthora ⟨symbol⟩ agem in the enharmonic. scale of the Third Tone, producing the desired lowering of Zo by a semi-tone.

Concerning Modulation

    We saw in the preceeding chapter that phthorai produce a change or movement from one scale to another, or from one tone to another. We call that change modulation. Modulation is extremely necessary in singing for two important reasons:

1.   For variety in singing, which, if we were to remain for an extended time in the same scale, it would become monotonous.

2.   Through modulations we are able to restate more expressively the meaning of the hymn's text.

As in western, liniar music, a modulation can be either passing (temporary) or definitive. But usually psaltic music returns, after a modulation, to the original tone.

In psaltic music modulations are accomplished with the help of phthorai, in the same way western music uses accidentals.

TEMPORARY MODULATIONS
From Di of Tone II to all the scales of the other tones

NOTE I: From the above examples, we can see that the note Di (Sol) the vasis of the second tone, is a central note in the formation of all the scales (look at the disdiaponate scale which begins on low Di (Sol)).

NOTE II: It has been said that the second tone is also a 'semi-chromatic' tone, because the movement of the melody is made almost exclusively in the second tetracord, leaving the first tetracord large possibilities to bind itself to the other tones through modulation.

KATAVASIA OF THE HOLY CROSS
"The Senseless Decree" (Ode 7)

Tone VIII   ὦ, Νι Τ

după A. PANN și N. IONESCU

The sense-less de-cree of the pa-gan and wick- ed

ty - rant dis-con-cert - ed the - peop-le

by breath-ing forth- ter -ri — — ble threats

and blas-phe- my - hate- ful to God; how-ev- er

the three child- ren could- not be fright- ened

by neith- er the - fur - y of wild beasts nor

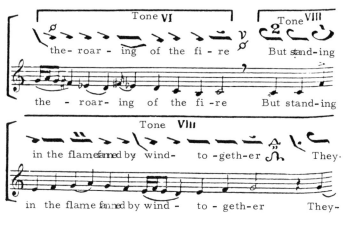

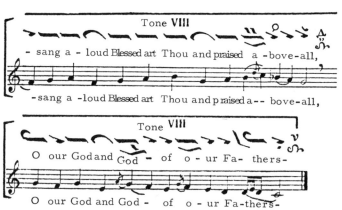

Final General Observations

Keeping in mind the numerous changes which psaltic music semiography
has undergone over time, and also the different interpretations given to
various vocal and especially consonant signs; and similarly keeping in
mind the way in which the text was reproduced and set, accompanied by
the psaltic notation in the present publications, we make the following
necessary observations:

1.   On the Petasti

Taking into consideration the variant theories and interpretations
of the petasti, but especially taking into consideration the fact that in
today's practice a simple pestasti (without a clasma or other psaltic sign)
is always executed by ascending one step with a pronounced accent, we have
adopted the definition given by most psaltic composers: "The petasti
ascends one step, sing it more accentuatedly."

Likewise, in all the transpositions from psaltic to liniar notation
published up until the present by competant composers, the petasti is
transposed by ascending one step accentuatedly. This is the way it is
found in "The Angel Cried" by Macarie, and harmonized by D.G. Kiriac;
and in "It is Truly Meet" in Tones V and VI by Stefanache Popescu, (In
The Book of Ecclesiastical Hymns, compiled by Nifon N. Ploesteanu); in
Hymn of the Divine Liturgy published by I. Popescu-Pasarea; in the trans-
position of different ecclesiastical hymns and their harmonizations by
G. Cucu, I. Chirescu and others; as well as in those published by the
Greek musical review Μουσική of Constantinople (1912), etc.

Observations on Consonants

The execssive use of consonants, as can be seen in many of the psaltic hymns published up until now, is to the detrement of the melodic beauty of our ecclesiastical hymns. For this reason, in the examples in this book they are employed only when necessary and being careful not to destroy the beauty of the hymns.

In this category is included: varia, psifiston, antichenoma: the consonants which through their frequent use often destort the melodic line. In an attempt to maintain the beauty of these hymns, we have used them only where the sense of the text requires them.

The Simple Antichenoma (without an apli) especially is found used frequently and often without any reason. Keeping in mind that in practice its execution, especially in the minor grace notes, is hardly able to be perceived, much less to be heard, being unable to be executed by a group of singers, it has been often used with an apli, but is used alone only when there is a need.

Similarly, the varia has been used most often in the formulae of cadences, when it is followed by a note with a clasma.

Concerning the use of the psifiston, which in transcription is always translated by either a long or short arpeggio, as may be the case. This is used rarely, keeping in mind that its frequent repetition is detremental to the hymns.

Otherwise, we should remember that the use of psaltic consonants, as with the use of different ornamentations in western liniar music, vary in interpretation from age to age and even from composer to composer.

133

3. Observations about the Text

The writing of the text under the psaltic and liniar notes was made
in conformity with the grammatical rules observed today by all the pub-
lishers of liniar music. Likewise the repetition of vowels under all
the notes which prolong them as was the custom in earlier psaltic publications, has been avoided. If a vowel was prolonged and not repeated,
then this prolongation was shown by a dash as in western publications.

4. Observation about Rythmn

a) In the area of rythmn of psaltic hymns we have seen that in these
hymns we encounter notes with a value of 1, 2, 3, and 4 beats. Similarly
we encounter 2, 3 and 4 notes to one beat, etc. All these rythmic formulae
are sufficient for the execution of ecclesiastical hymns, which is the
object of this study. More complicated rythmic formulae formed by the
combination of digorga and trigorga with an apli, dipli, or tripi, are
subject material for another special study.

b) As a complement to that which was said in the chapter:
"Concerning Tempo," we add: Therefore the stihirarica tempo which indicates
a slow tempo, has been render in liniar music by the following terms:
Andante and Larghetto; in the stihi of Vespers and Matins of the Third
and Seventh Tones which have a more lively tempo, we have adopted the
term: Andantino.

PSALTIC ORTHOGRAPHY - According to Macarie and Anton Pann

<u>Appendix</u>

From the first part of this book we have seen that psaltic music has four types of signs, called: vocal, temporal, consonant, and phthoral.

The most important of these, without which we would be unable to sing anything, are the vocal signs. The other signs merely embellish and beautify the melodies which are outlined by the vocal signs.

For this reason, in this section on psaltic orthography, we will take each of the ten vocal signs, in order, and we will show the manner in which they can be written and embellished both with other vocal signs and with the other temporal, consonant, and phthoral signs.

We therefore begin with the first vocal sign:

     I.   ISON: ╰──

The ison can be written both by itself and with other vocal signs. It is written alone when the sound which it represents should be sung simply, without any accent.

Ex. 1.

    1) With Vocal Signs

The ison is written only with the oligon and the petasti. This is when it is assisted by these two vocal signs, thusly:

    a)   Assisted by an oligon. Written thusly when the syllable of the word under it is slightly accented, after which another ison follows and then a vocal sign of descent.

Ex. 2.

b)   Assisted by a petasti. Written thusly when the syllable
under it requires more accentuation, after which a vocal sign of descent
follows.

Ex. 3.

NOTE: If the petasti has a clasma, then two vocal signs of descent
must follow:

Ex. 3 b

2)   The ison can be written with each of the temporal signs
except for the argon. The gorgon is written either above or below it;
the clasma above it; and the apli with its various compounds, below it.

We should make the following observation with regard to how the ison
is written with the apli and its compounds.

a)   The ison takes an apli (·), only when it is written under an
antichenoma, the text having a syllable which is being elongated by a
vocal sign of descent.

Ex. 4.

b)   If the syllable is not elongated, then the antichenoma with
apli is replaced with a clasma.

Ex. 5.

c)   The ison is written with the other compounds of the apli
(" , ''' , etc.) only if it has below it an eteron preceded by a varia,
and the syllable of the text is elongated further.

Ex. 6

136

d)   But if there is a new syllable of the text under the vocal

sign of descent which follows the ison, then the compounds of the apli

are written without an eteron and varia.

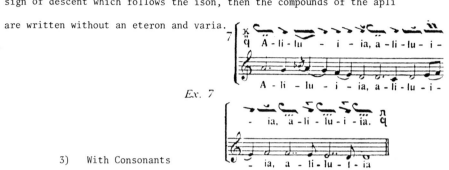

Ex. 7

3)   With Consonants

The ison can be written with each of the consonants thusly:

a)   With a varia. In addition to its use shown above in 2c, it

can also be used with a varia when a vocal sign of descent follows the

ison and the text has the same syllable being elongated.

Ex. 8.

NOTE: When the vocal sign of descent is an hyporoe, a varia is

written only if both descending notes of the hyporoe are on the up-beat

by means of a digorgon; or if an apostrophos follows the hyporoe and

all the notes are on the up-beat by means of a trigorgon.

Ex. 9.

An exception to this is made at the end of a musical phrase, when it is possible for an hyporoe to have only a gorgon. (Ex. 10a). But often it also appears without a gorgon (Ex. 10b).

b) With an Omalon. An ison is written with an omalon when it is preceeded by either another ison or an oligon. It can either have a gorgon or not. It also must elongate a syllable which begins either on the preceeding ison or oligon. And this group of notes must also be preceeded by a varia which gives more emphasis to the effect of the omalon.

Ex. 11.

c) With a Psifiston. When the ison is followed by two or more descending notes and the idea of the text requires the ison to be sung with greater emphasis, then the ison is written with a psifiston.

Ex. 12.

But if the ison has a clasma, then two of more descending notes must follow, and at least the first of these descending notes must have a clasma.

Ex. 13.

d)   With an eteron. In addition to the uses of the ison with the eteron in conjunction with temporal signs (dipli, tripli, etc.) shown above (I,2,c), the ison also makes use of the eteron in the following instance:

When an ison or an oligon with a syllable or an elongation of a syllable is followed by another ison which elongates the preceeding syllable, and the idea of the text requires a slight modulation upward between the two notes of the same step, then these notes are bound together by an eteron.

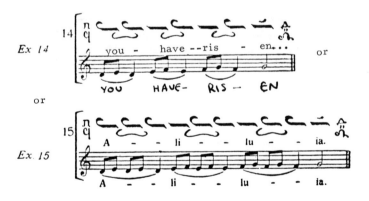

Ex 14

or

or

Ex. 15

e)   With phthoral signs. The ison can be written with any
of the phthorai, according to the wish of the composer. Phthorai can
be written both above and below the ison, in the most convenient
place, keeping in mind the location of the other signs: temporal
or consonant which have their given place.

Ex. 17.

It should be noted that the accidental sharp (σ) and flats (ρ)
continue to be written above and below the ison, respectively.

II.   The Oligon

The oligon uses the vocal, temporal, consonant and phthoral signs
in the same way as the ison, of course keeping its destinctive characteristic.

In general its function is to ascend one step in a simple fashion.   It
can be written either alone or with other psaltic signs.

It is written alone when the melody ascends one step at a time and
a new syllable is under each note.

Ex. 18.

In hymns with slower tempo (heruvika, axions, etc.) the oligon can
also be used to elongate a syllable:

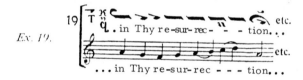

Ex. 19.

Among the vocal signs, the oligon uses the kentimata most frequently and it can be written either above or below the oligon.

a)   The kentimata is written under the oligon when the syllable of the text ascends in pairs of notes.

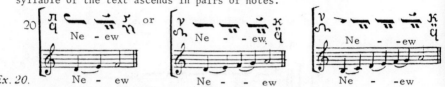

Ex. 20.

When a two syllable word ascends an odd number of notes step by step, then only the first syllable is used to ascend with.

Ex. 21

b)   Oligon followed by kentimata. Kentimata are written alone after an oligon, when after having ascended step by step there follows descending notes of similar duration. The final kentimata, however, is written above the oligon with a psifiston below.

Ex. 22.

c) Kentimata above an oligon. Kentimata can be written above an oligon either with or without a gorgon, when the syllable below the oligon requires an ascending note; after which either an ison or descending note follows.

Ex. 23   for Thou a - lone art- Ho-ly   or

for Thou a- lone art Ho- ly

Ex. 24   Thou a- lone art - the- Lord-

Thou a- lone art - the- Lord - ···

One can also place two or three oligons with kentimatas one after the other, if an ison follows afterward.   *Examplu* 25, 26

Ex 25   glo-ry to - - - Thee-   or

glo-ry to - - - Thee-

Ex 26   glo-ry to Thee - ee   etc.

glo- ry- to Thee - ee - ee - ee --

<u>General Observation</u>

The oligon, in addition to combination with the vocal signs ⌣, ᾿ ⌣, can also be placed below an ison and all the vocal signs of descent, in which case they are all sung a little more accentuatedly. (See page 24.)

2. Oligon with Temporal Signs

The oligon can be written with all the temporal signs according to the following rules:

a) **With a clasma.** Usually the clasma is written above the oligon in this way: ![sign] . However, if the oligon has a kentima or an ipsile above it, then the clasma is written below the oligon in this way: ![sign] ![sign] Only when the oligon has a psifiston below it, is the clasma written next to the kentima.

Ex 27

To Thee O - - Lord

To Thee O - -Lord

b) **With the gorgon and its composites.** The oligon can always be written with a gorgon and its composites, except when the oligon has a psifiston or an omalon, which do not go with a gorgon. In general, the gorgon is written above the oligon, but is written below when the oligon begins a musical phrase. However, we must always keep in mind its most suitable positioning when confronting consonants or phthorai whose position is firmly regulated.

Ex. 28

the sing-ing of the an-gel-ic - ho ⸗sts...

the sing-ing of- the an-gel-ic - ho - sts...

c) **With the apli and its compounds.** The oligon is written with these according to the same rules as for the ison (I,2, a and c).

d) **The argon and diargon** are written only above the oligon, which has a kentimata below and does not take any other consonants except an omalon or a psifiston.

Exemplu : 29

29

We - who — like ___ Che-ru- bi - im

We - who- - like - - Che-ru- bi - - im

3.　Oligon with consonants

The oligon, like the ison, makes use of all the consonants, in this way:

a)　The oligon preceeded by a varia is written when a descending sign with a gorgon follows it extending the same syllable.

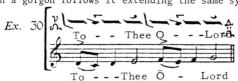

b)　The oligon with a varia and eteron, will be examine later in this chapter at: 3,G.

c)　Oligon with omalon. When the sense of the text requires a greater accentuation, the oligon takes a clasma or an argon and is written with an omalon, and is followed by an apostrophos also with a clasma.

NOTE 1:　However, often the additional beat of the apostrophos with clasma can be replaced by a kentimata which follows immediately after the apostrophos; the effect of the omalon continues to refer to the oligon.

NOTE 2:　An oligon with a clasma can take an omalon, in which case a simple apostrophos without any temporal sign follows.

145

NOTE 3: But if the melodic sense of the text does not require an oligon with clasma modulated by an omalon, then do not place an omalon underneath the oligon, although the apostrophos with a clasma follows.

d) An oligon with a psifiston, is written:

1) When a vocal sign of descent of the same duration follows.

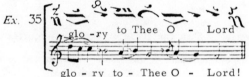

NOTE: But if the descending sign which follows has a lesser duration, then the oligon with psifiston is replaced by a petasti with clasma in this way:

2) When an oligon is followed by a continuous elaphron, then the oligon takes a psifiston.

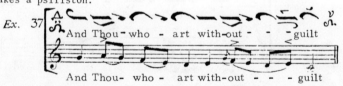

3) When, after an oligon with a kentimata above it, two apostrophi with the same syllable follow, in the place of a varia, an oligon is written, with a psifiston.

4) When two or more descending notes follow an oligon, and the first of these has the same duration as the oligon, then the oligon takes a psifiston.

Ex. 39

e) Oligon with an antichenoma. An oligon can take an antichenoma, when we desire that the step be sung with a quick upward modulation, but without a new syllable which would require a kentimata. In addition, one or more descending steps must then follow (apostrophos or elaphron) similarly without a new syllable.

Exemplele 40 și 41.

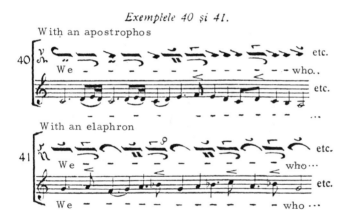

NOTE 1: If after an oligon with an antichenoma which is followed by an apostrophos, there is an oligon followed by an elaphron, then the antichenoma is placed only on the oligon which is followed by the apostrophos.

Ex. 42.

147

<u>NOTE 2</u>: If under the elaphron there is a new syllable, the oligon
cannot take an antichenoma, but is written simply, like this:

Ex. 43.

f)   An oligon which has an antichenoma with apli. As with
the ison, the oligon is able to use the antichenoma with apli, if the
descending note which follows it has the same syllable.

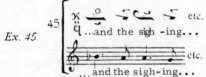

<u>NOTE</u>: When the descending note which follows has a new syllable, the
oligon is written with a clasma, as described with the ison (I,2,b).

Ex. 45

g)   <u>Oligon with eteron</u>. An oligon preceeded by a varia takes an
eteron:

1)   When it is followed by a descending note with a gorgon, bound
to another oligon by the elongation of a syllable.

Ex. 46.

2)   This is also the case when, after the descending note with
gorgon, another oligon with a kentimata follows having a gorgon on top,
and this is followed by a descending note or an ison.

3)   The oligon also takes an eteron, followed by a descending
note with the same syllable, when its duration is prolonged by two, three,
or more beats by means of a dipli, tripli, etc.

h)   With phthorai the oligon follows the same rules as the ison
(I,3,e).

III. PETASTI ⌣

In addition to what was said in the first part of the book relative
to the petasti both alone and with clasma, we would like to explain the
following orthographic rules pertaining to the petasti.

The petasti is written alone or with other vocal signs, temporal signs,
consonants and phthoral signs.

When it is written alone it ascends one step like an oligon, however,
in a slightly more accented fashion. This is why it is always written
over the accented syllable of a word in the text. After it one or two
descending signs follow. The petasti is used then when we have need of an
accentuated step upward during the course of the melody, and after which
follows a descending note with or without a clasma.

NOTE: After the petasti one cannot place: an ison, nor any of the vocal signs of accent; neither can one place two or more petasti one after the other, rather a vocal sign of descent always follows.

Ex. 49.

O Thou who art the ful-fill-ment

1. With Vocal Signs

All the vocal signs (both combination and assisted) except for the kentimata, can be written with the petasti; they receive the petasti's characteristic accentuation.

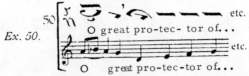

Ex. 50.

O great pro-tec- tor of...

NOTE 1: When the melody ascends step by step, and the final ascending note has a clasma, and two descending vocal signs follow, then the final ascending note must be a petasti, like this:

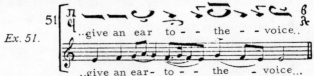

Ex. 51.

..give an ear- to - - the - voice...

NOTE 2: If after the final ascending note there immediately follows an apostrophos and an hyporoe, then the final ascending sign must again be a petasti, like this:

Exemplul 52

Now - - - - - - - - - let___

2. With Temporal Signs

From among the temporal signs, the petasti takes a clasma and an apli with antichenoma. But it never takes a gorgon and its compounds, nor the argon and the diargon, nor the dipli, tripli, etc.

a) When a petasti has a clasma then two or more descending notes or a descending note with a clasma must follow.

NOTE: A petasti with clasma, followed by a single descending note without clasma, is never written except in the following cadence formula:

b) If the petasti has an apli with antichenoma, it must be followed by a descending note with a gorgon.

Exemplul 57

3. With Consonants

The petasti takes only the varia and the psifiston from among the consonants.

a) A varia is placed before a petasti only when the petasti has an antichenoma with apli, as in example 57 above or like this:

b) The psifiston is written below a petasti only in the cadence formula shown in example 56 above.

NOTE: The antichenoma is written below the petasti only in conjunction with the apli, as we saw in Section 2,b, Ex. 57 above.

4. With Phthorai

The petasti takes all the phthoral signs, sharps, and flats following the same rules as the oligon.

IV. THE KENTIMATA ⑁

The kentimata can be written either alone or with other vocal signs, temporal signs and consonants. It can never be used to start a syllable, but is always used to elongate a syllable (that is after another vocal sign which can take a new syllable). It is never written alone at the beginning or the end of a musical phrase, but is placed after other vocal signs to which it is bound.

Ex. 59.

1. With Vocal Signs

The kentimata can be written in conjunction with all vocal signs
except the petasti or the kentima. However, it is usually joined to
the ison or the oligon.

a) With the ison. The kentimata is never written above nor
below the ison, but only along side it. After the kentimata neither a
descending nor ascending sign can follow, but only an ison.

Exemplul 60

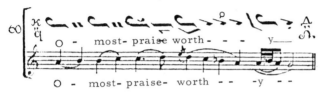

b) With the oligon. The kentimata is written with the oligon in
three ways: above, below and after the oligon.

1. It is written above the oligon when a vocal sign of descent
follows.

Ex. 61.

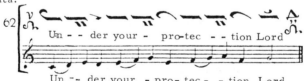

2. It is written below the oligon when the syllable which began on
the preceeding note continues, finishing its ascent on the oligon above
the kentimata.

Exemplul 62

Or if it continues to another note.

Ex. 63.

153

3. After the oligon. The kentimata is written after the oligon when the syllable which began under that oligon is elongated by the kentimata and the melody continues to climb with another syllable.

Ex. 64.

NOTE 1: However, if after the last kentimata, an ison above a petasti follows in place of a vocal sign of ascent, then the kentimata is not written after the oligon but above it.

Ex. 65.

NOTE 2: But when the text has only two syllables (ex. mankind) then the first kentimata is written under the oligon, and the final one is changed into an oligon.

Ex. 66.

2. With Temporal Signs

The kentimata takes only the gorgon with its compounds, and the argon and diargon from among the temporal signs, like this:

a) The kentimata can take the gorgon above or below it, according to where it is written, that is: it takes the gorgon below when it is wirtten after an oligon, and take it above when the kentimata is written above or below the oligon.

Ex. 67.

154

b)   The kentimata with an argon is always written like this:
he argon above the oligon with the kentimata below). The argon has
e function of a gorgon and clasma; that is, it takes the kentimata
 the upbeat, and one beat is added to the oligon.

Ex. 68.

3.   With Consonants

The kentimata makes use of the varia, omalon, and psifiston from among
e consonants.

a)   The varia is used by the kentimata only when it is on the
eat by means of a digorgon, trigorgon, etc.

Ex. 69.

b)   Omalon. The kentimata takes an omalon when it is placed after
ison and is on the upbeat by means of a digorgon.

Ex. 70.

NOTE: When a descending note immediately follows a kentimata, then
h the ison which is before this kentimata, and the kentimata are written
ve an oligon, like this:

Ex. 71.

c)   Psifiston. The kentimata takes a psifiston only when it is written above an oligon, elongating an accented syllable of the text. But a descending sign must follow it, according to the rule of oligon with psifiston, that is it must be of the same duration and descending step by step.

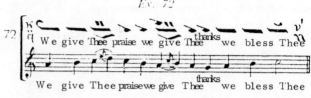

Ex. 72

4.   With Phthorai

The kentimata can take phthorai or any of the other signs of alteration, but this usage is rarely encountered.

V.   THE KENTIMA AND IPSILI

The usage of these two vocal signs is not regulated by special rules, rather they are bound by those regulating the oligon and petasti with which they are always written.

It should be noted, however, that to eliminate any confusion, a kentimata should not be placed after a kentima ⟨signs⟩ rather it should be written above an oligon, like this: ⟨sign⟩   [1] .

VI.   THE APOSTROPHOS

The apostrophos is written alone, if the descending note does not need to be accented. When it should be accented, however, it is written above other vocal signs, which are subject to the apostrophos. But in return they give it the necessary accentuation. Also, if one desires a special kind of expression on a certain note, then the vocal sign underneath the

---

[1] In Macarie's Theory Book (Chapter 7) there is also this arrangement ⟨sign⟩.   , but as he himself notes, this is very unusual and rarely encountered.

apostrophos can take a consonant, according to the expression desired, or
a phthora if the sense of the text requries a modulation.

The apostrophos can be written in these ways:

1)   Alone, its most usual use: *Ex. 73.*

2)   Above a vocal sign, excepting an ison, kentimata, or
hyporoe.   *Ex. 74.*

3)   With all of the temporal signs except for the argon

(see the preceeding example).

4.   Apostrophos with the Consonants

a)   An apostrophos alone can only take a varia or an antichenoma
with apli.

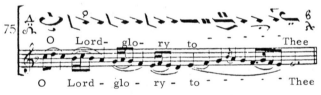

NOTE 1: Each pair of apostrophi, in the above example, is preceeded
by a varia. This is the orthographic rule, when a syllable is begun by
the first of the two apostrophi which form the pair. However, if the
syllable of the text begins on another note, then the first pair of
apostrophi no longer takes a varia.

Ex. 76.

<u>NOTE 2</u>: But if the apostrophi are not in pairs, and if the last one has a new syllable, then none of them takes a varia.

Ex. 77.

b) With the antichenoma and eteron. The apostrophos can only take the antichenoma with an apli, after which a descending note with a gorgon follows.

Ex. 78.

<u>NOTE 1</u>: When an apostrophos needs to be held longer, then in place of an antichenoma, one places an eteron with a dipli, tripli, etc., as we saw with the ison (I,2,c) and with the oligon (II,3,g).

Ex. 79.

<u>NOTE 2</u>: The apostrophos can take an eteron without a dipli, tripli, etc., if another apostrophos with the same syllable follows, after which either an ison or oligon follows.

Ex. 80.

c) The apostrophos can be written with the omalon and the psifiston like this:

Exemplul 81 şi 82.

Example with omalon

158

Example with a psifiston

82 Glo - ry - be to - Thee O - - Lord

Glo -ry - - be to - - Thee O - - - - Lord

5. With Phthorai

As we said above, the apostrophos can use phthorai when the text requires a change or modulation in the melody. In this case the apostrophos can take accidental sharps and flats, as well as any of the diatonic, chromatic, or enharmonic phthorai.

Ex. 83 ...and of the- hu - man- race...

...and of - the - hu - man - - race

Ex 84 ...lis-ten - to me O - - - Lord

...lis-ten to me O - - - - Lord

VII. THE HYPOROE

The hyporoe is not written at the beginning of a musical phrase, nor is it written alone, but always in conjunction with other vocal signs. This is because it is used only to elongate a syllable.

Ex. 85 day of - res-ur-rec-tion

day- of —res-ur-rec- tion

1) <u>With vocal signs</u>. It is written along side of all the
vocal signs, except for the kentimata, precisely when there is a need
for two progressive descending notes that elongate the syllable of
the preceeding note.

a)   The hyporoe can be written above an oligon when a kentimata
follows it, and when two or more descending notes follow the kentimata.

b)   It can also be written above a petasti with clasma when the
second note of the hyporoe requires an accentuation. Another hyporoe must
follow.

It should be noted that the second beat of the hyporoe can not be
represented by an apli. Rather it takes a petasti with clasma to accomplish this task.

2)   With temporal signs. From among the temporal signs, the hyporoe
uses only the apli and gorgon with their compounds:

a)   The apli and its compounds. The hyporoe can take neither an
argon nor clasma. When the second descending note needs to be extended
by two or more beats, then an apli, dipli, etc. is placed below it.

b)   The gorgon and its compounds are written above the hyporoe like this: the gorgon has its effect on the first descending note and the preceeding note; but if both descending notes should be taken in the upbeat then it takes a digorgon; and likewise with the trigorgon, etc. With the digorgon, trigorgon, etc., other vocal signs will also begin to be affected by them.

3.   With consonants. The hyporoe is never written with a psifiston, and it rarely appears with the other consonants.

a)   It can be written with a varia, when it is assisted by a petasti.

NOTE: The final descending note of the hyporoe receives the effect from both the petasti with clasma and from the varia.

b)   It is written with an omalon when the final descending note of the hyporoe and the ison which must follow it, should be sung with its characteristic modulation.

c)   The antichenoma with apli can be placed on the second descending note to give it its characteristics leaping quality, like this:

Ex. 94

Earth - - - - - ly...

Earth - - - - - ly...

d)   With an eteron. The hyporoe can be written with an eteron when: the second descending note is followed by an ison, they are both on the same syllable, and they need to be sung with a slight modulation.

Ex. 95

O - - - Lord

O - - - Lord

NOTE: When the second note of the hyporoe needs to be held longer, and a descending note with gorgon follows it, then the eteron is written with a dipli, tripli, etc.

Ex. 96

A - - - li - lu - ia. _____

A - - - li - lu - ia. ____

4)   Phthorai and other accidentals can be placed abov   hyporoe affecting its first descending note, or below, affecting its second descendi note. However, the most usual usage is the later.

VIII. THE ELAPHRON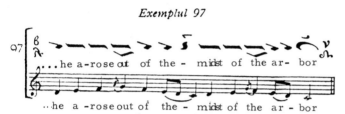

The elaphron can be placed at the beginning, middle or end of a musical
phrase. As we have previously seen, the elaphron, when written alone,
descends two steps transgressively. But if an apostrophos is written
immediately after it (continuous elaphron), then the apostrophos is sung
on the upbeat, as though it had a gorgon, and the elaphron on the down beat,
however descending only one step. The effect is similar to the hyporoe
with gorgon. The difference between them, however, is in the manner of
singing the text: the hyporoe has the same syllable for both descending
notes, while the continuous elaphron takes a different syllable on each
of the two notes.

Exemplul 97

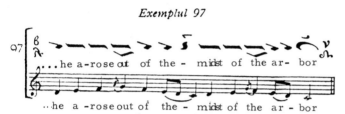

...he a-rose at of the - midst of the ar- bor

..he a -rose out of the - midst of the ar - bor

However, if the apostrophos is separated from the elaphron by a comma or by a space, each is sung according to its own rules: the apostrophos descends one step, and the elaphron two steps, each with one beat.

Ex. 98.

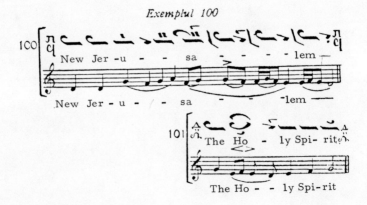

1. The elaphron can be written alone or assisted by the oligon and petasti.

a) As with the apostrophos and the hyporoe, the elaphron is sung without accent when written alone.

Ex. 99

b) When written assisted by an oligon or petasti, then it is sung more accentuately or more lively.

Exemplul 100

2.   The Elaphron with Temporal Signs

The elaphron takes only the clasma, and the gorgon with its compounds from among the temporal signs. They can be written above or below, according to the most suitable location, and keeping in mind other signs whose position is regulated, as we saw also with the oligon (II,2,a&b). An argon, however, is never placed on the elaphron.

NOTE: When the melody requires an ison with gorgon, immediately preceeding a continuous elaphron (i.e., ison, apostrophos, elaphron), then the ison and the apostrophos are both taken on the upbeat, as though they had a digorgon.

This example can be analyzed like this:

3.   Elaphron with consonants

The elaphron uses all of the consonants in the following ways: varia, preceeding the elaphron; omalon, antichenoma, and eteron, located directly under it; and the psifiston also underneath it, but with an oligon above the psifiston. In each of these cases the elaphron takes the effect of the consonant placed on it.

Here is one example for each consonant's use with the elaphron:

1) Elaphron with varia:

A - rise O Lord give as- sis-tance to - us...

2) Elaphron with varia and omalon:

3) Elaphron with antichenoma and apli:

4) Elaphron with eteron (combined with dipli and tripli and preceeded by varia):

5) Elaphron assisted by oligon with psifiston:

4. The Elaphron with Phthorai and Accidentals

The elaphron can take any phthorai or accidentals both above (as in Ex. 107 above) and below it, as with the apostrophos (VI. 5).

Exemplul 108

108
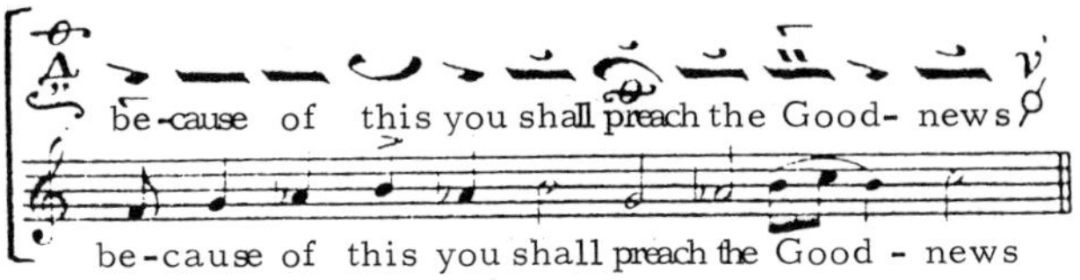

IX. HAMILI

The final vocal sign in psaltic notation is the hamili. It can be written alone or assisted by other vocal signs as we have already seen.

The hamili is never written at the beginning of a hymn. It is also the most infrequently used of all the vocal signs, used only when the sense of text calls for a drop in the melody.

109
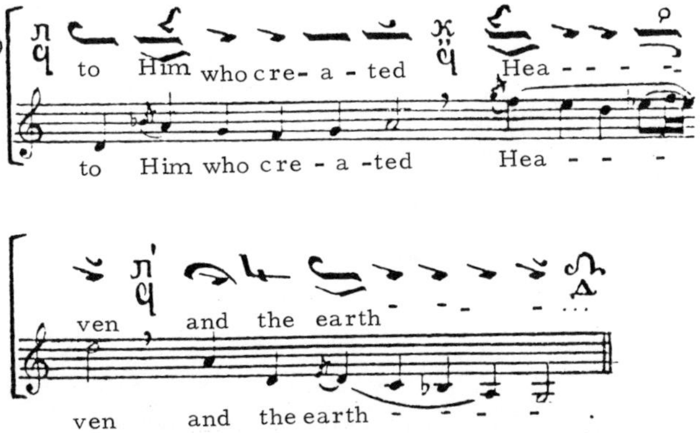

In general, the hamili uses the same orthographic rules as the elaphron, except, of course, for the continuous elaphron ( ), which does not pertain to the hamili.

Here is an example of a hamili combined with an apostrophos, clasma, and a sharp:

Exemplul 110

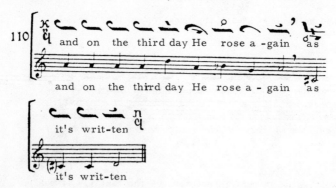